MORE YANKEE YARNS

By the same author
YANKEE YARNS

MORE
YANKEE
YARNS

by

Alton H. Blackington

Illustrated
with photographs

DODD, MEAD & COMPANY
NEW YORK, 1956

© 1956 by Alton H. Blackington

Library of Congress Catalog Card Number: 56-10054

To Alice

Printed in the United States of America
by The Cornwall Press, Inc., Cornwall, N. Y.

FOREWORD

As in my first book, *Yankee Yarns,* these stories are the result of my years of work in New England as a newspaper photographer and feature writer, and as a narrator of stories on radio and television. I was very young when I realized that a story anywhere acted on me like a magnet. I wanted to go where the story was, hear all about it, talk to those who knew the facts, make notes, and take pictures. I was never content until I had written the Yarn or told people about it.

That is how the tales in this book came into being. They were gathered in my wanderings through this land of mine which is the home of folks whom the world calls Yankees. These have been happy wanderings; a life more interesting than anything else I can imagine doing.

If you who scan the pages of this volume find the stories anywhere near as interesting in the reading as I did in the getting of them, you will be rewarded. And this will make me happy, for to a story-teller there is no satisfaction quite equal to the thrill of a responsive audience.

There is a unity to this group of stories not immediately apparent. Taken from every nook and corner of New England as they are, and describing a significant time in the lives of widely different people, each one presents some typical feature of the life and people of our region. The widely different characters and episodes in these stories serve to demonstrate aspects of the Yankee which make him interesting to readers the world over: his versatility and unpredictability, his ingenuity and persistence, his never-ending variety. Whatever else he may be, a Yankee is never a bore!

So, folks, here are some More Yankee Yarns. Happy reading! I promise you more some future day.

Alton H. Blackington

Beverly Farms, Massachusetts

ACKNOWLEDGMENTS

In addition to those mentioned in the text, I wish to thank the following for their help: J. Sanger Attwill, Harlan G. Barrett, Fred R. Brine, Laurence B. Brown, Mrs. Lincoln Colcord, Charles H. P. Copeland, E. P. Davenport, Arnold C. Dickinson, Ernest S. Dodge, Fanny Hardy Eckstorm, Harry E. Erskine, Helen J. Estes, Kingdon Harvey, Charles F. Haywood, Mr. and Mrs. Thomas Mason Hill, Harland Little, Mrs. John Montgomery, Malcolm D. Pearson, Neal Powers, John M. Richardson, Alvin F. Sortwell, Jr., Edward Rowe Snow, "Chief" Stanwood, Ernest S. Tucker, Mrs. John J. Veale, Carl Warton; Chamber of Commerce, Barton, Vermont; Boston *Globe, Herald, Post;* Essex Institute, Salem; The Millicent Library, Fairhaven, Massachusetts; New Bedford *Standard Times;* The New Hampshire Historical Society, Concord; Peabody Museum of Salem; Orleans County Historical Society, Orleans, Vermont; *Reader's Digest;* Widener Library, Harvard University; *Yankee* Magazine.

CONTENTS

CONTENTS

ILLUSTRATIONS

(Photographic supplement follows page 86)

HEROIC ESCAPADES

THE British fleet, sent to New England to subdue the rebel Colonies, dropped anchor off Newport, Rhode Island, on December 1, 1776, finding that peaceful island community defenseless and practically deserted. All the able-bodied men had enlisted with the local militia and had gone to Tiverton, or had marched off to fight in Massachusetts or New York. Only a handful of young and old men, sickly inhabitants and Tories, were left on the island to tend shops and stores, till the fields and guard the women and children.

The fleet, commanded by Lord Percy, consisted of the frigates *Lark*, *Diamond* and *Juno*, with their tenders, transports and sloops of war. Below decks was a formidable force of 10,000 well-seasoned English soldiers and Hessians in command of General Henry Clinton.

The first of the regiments disembarked at Long Wharf on December 8 and took possession of Newport. The main body landed at Coddington's Cove on December 9, marched to Gould's Hill where they encamped for the night and moved into Newport the next day, grabbing whatever took their fancy from homes along the way.

From ten to fifty of these men were quartered with each family, making life unbearable, and they stayed there until the first warm days of spring when they moved into tents. Horses were stabled in the Newport churches, the pews of which had been ripped out and burned; only Trinity was spared and reserved as a place of worship.

Fortifications thrown up by the Yankees, then abandoned when this large naval force appeared, were seized by the enemy, enlarged, strengthened and garrisoned. New redoubts and additional breastworks were built at strategic points.

In the spring of 1777, General Clinton and Lord Percy sailed for New York, leaving the British troops in Newport in charge of General Richard Prescott, the most hated man who ever wore the king's uniform. Haughty, high-handed and tyrannical, Prescott treated all the Newport Yankees with disdain and cruelty. Innocent persons were slapped into prison without a trial, others were beaten, several were killed.

When the soldiers complained that their tents were too cold, Prescott pointed to the fine shade trees and shouted, "Cut them down! They'll warm your tents!" When the trees had been reduced to ashes, he suggested that wooden sidewalks make fine fuel. He even dispatched a group of Hessians to the town cemeteries to pull up wooden crosses and grave markers, and clapped his fat, soft hands in glee when he saw them go up in smoke. Wooden fences which for years had marked the boundaries between farms like-wise went into the flames, a loss which later caused great confusion to the owners.

Every day General Prescott waddled around Newport on a tour of inspection. As he sauntered down Spring Street toward the State House, he found the way rough, unpaved and muddy. Summoning a work party, he ordered all the stone doorsteps removed from in front of the houses and placed in the middle of the street. That gave him a fine, level, dry place to walk, and all townspeople were warned to keep off.

Prescott decreed that every woman and child in Newport should make a low curtsy when he approached them and that every male citizen should remove his hat and remain bareheaded as long as "His Majesty" was in sight. As many of Newport's citizens were Quakers, this was especially offensive to them, but any failure to comply meant severe punishment. If Prescott came upon a group talking, passing the time of day, he shook his cane and yelled, "Disperse, ye vile rebels!"

Newport folks were much relieved when General Prescott announced that he was moving his headquarters from the John Bannister house on Pelham Street to the Overing farm, five miles out of town on the old West Road. Overing, a dignified Quaker, was much displeased, but as he was powerless, the British tyrant took over the farm.

In June, a patriot named Coffin escaped from the island and was taken at once to the Yankee camp at Tiverton, where he was welcomed by Colonel William Barton.

Barton, a native of Warren, Rhode Island, had enlisted under General Artemus Ward in Cambridge just after the battle of Bunker Hill. He had served with honor under Israel Putnam and had met George Washington and Henry Knox at Dorchester Heights. When the Rhode Island Assembly had sent to Massachusetts for men to organize military companies for the protection of Providence, Bristol and Newport, William Barton was appointed to command them. He was an aggressive patriot, and for months he had longed to make an independent strike against the British.

On questioning Coffin and also a British deserter, Barton got such a minute description of Prescott's quarters on the second floor of the Overing house that he felt he could find them blindfolded. He was thoroughly familiar with every part of the island, having been stationed there a few months before. Day after day he mulled over the idea of sneaking across to Newport and grabbing the British general as his prisoner.

He would need help, of course; so confidentially he made his scheme known to five of his officers whom he could trust. They endorsed the plan and begged to go with him.

Night after night as Barton walked along the shore in Tiverton, telescope in hand, he would look out across the dark water toward enemyheld Newport, trying to decide the best way for his boats to go. There were three enemy frigates lying at anchor between his camp and the island, and Barton knew that his men would have to row or drift practically under their bows. If discovered, they would surely be shot at; if captured, they would be hanged.

Nevertheless he decided to take the chance, and one evening he ordered his regiment to be paraded, and addressed the men quietly. He said he was about to undertake a dangerous mission against the enemy. He asked for forty volunteers. Every man in the regiment stepped forward! It was not easy to pick out a few from so many, but Barton chose only the men who could row and sail a boat, who could shoot straight, men who would do as they were told and keep their mouths shut.

They shoved off the next night, July 4, 1777 (just one year after the Declaration of Independence). A storm was coming up, and the sky and water were black as ink, but they proceeded safely for two miles until they entered Mount Hope Bay. Here the wind sprang up, spray dashed in their faces and the whaleboats became unmanageable. As vivid shafts of lightning split the heavens and thunder rolled around them, the boats became separated and lost all contact. The weather was so wild that night that they didn't reach their rendezvous until nearly five o'clock the next afternoon. It had taken twenty-six hours to cross storm-tossed Mount Hope Bay, but finally they all gathered at camp near Bristol, and after drying out and partaking of hot coffee, they took up their oars again for the short distance to Hog Island.

From that isolated spot they had a clear view of Narragansett Bay and the flickering campfires of the British soldiers on shore. Standing under the stars, Barton told his forty volunteers where they were headed and what he intended to do.

[5]

Then they returned to Bristol, where they were held up by more bad weather. On the evening of July 9, Barton gave final instructions, concluding with, "There will be no smoking, no drinking, no talking. Now, men, let us pray to the good Lord to guide and watch over us." Each soldier respectfully raised his hat, then hastily replaced it and took his station.

Silent as ghosts the five whaleboats glided between the British warships, where sentries were plainly seen on the decks and their "All's Well!" was clearly heard.

By skillful maneuvering the boatmen worked up close to the shore and grounded their craft in a cove about a mile and a half from the Overing farm. They left one man to guard each boat, and the rest, with Barton leading, hastened toward the house. Right beside the colonel was his faithful personal servant, a colored youth, Guy Watson, who was to play an important role in the capture of General Prescott.

Cautiously and carefully they went up a slight rise, then down through a gully, and came out just in front of Prescott's headquarters. As expected, they were halted by a British sentry who asked, "Friend or foe?" and upon being told "Friend," said, "Advance and give the password!"

"Password!" hissed Barton. "We haven't any password. We're looking for deserters. Let us go by!" As the sentry lowered his musket, a cloak was thrown over his head and he was dragged off and gagged. As previously arranged, the house was quickly surrounded and the guards silenced.

Barton and Guy Watson pushed open the front door

[6]

and dashed upstairs. The first door was fastened and there was no light from within; the same was true of the second and third. But at the far end of the hall candlelight showed under a door and Barton tried the knob. That door was bolted too. At a signal, Guy Watson backed, lowered his head like a billy goat and smashed into the wooden panels, splinters flying in all directions. Colonel Barton reached through the hole, shoved back the bolt, and the two went in.

There, swaying drunkenly on the edge of his bed, was General Prescott, stark naked, trying to get into his linen nightgown. His men had captured a Yankee sloop returning to Providence with a cargo of rum, and he had been celebrating.

"General Prescott! You're under arrest!" said Barton. "Come along and don't speak a word!" Before the General knew what was happening, he was dragged downstairs and turned over to Yankee soldiers who were instructed, "Take him through the field!"

Prescott protested feebly and pleaded for his shirt and pants, but he was hustled off, the sharp stubble cutting into his bare feet and the long blackberry brambles raking his portly limbs.

At the shore, he was helped into No. 1 boat, where he sat shivering and shaking until Barton kindly tossed his own cloak around him.

As they pushed off, the men heard shouts of alarm and shots, and a few moments later the boom of a cannon rousing the sleeping countryside and the ships in the channel.

The exultant Yankees rowed for dear life and were soon beyond gunshot from their enemies on shore. Behind them, bugles blared, drums beat and a dozen beacon fires flared against the night sky. Musket balls fell harmlessly in the water, too far astern to do any damage.

Directly ahead lay the British frigates that were blockading the channel. Barton's men, with carefully muffled oars, slipped under the stern of one huge warship and the bowsprit of another, barely out of sight of the sailors who were now scampering over the decks.

As the five whaleboats passed between Conanicut and Prudence Islands, the sky lightened, turned pink and then golden as the sun rose over the horizon, revealing on shore a panorama of blackened beams and charred timbers of roofless homes: the trampled fields and abandoned wrecks of farms which the British and Hessians had devastated.

General Prescott was quite sober by now, aided no doubt by the salt spray that splashed over him. It was a relief to all of them when at last, around nine in the morning of July 10, the whaleboats touched the shore of Warwick Neck. Barton escorted his prisoner to comfortable quarters at the fort, assuring him that he would be treated as befitted his rank, ordered a hot breakfast and secured for him a pair of trousers.

Prescott respectfully asked for his own garments instead; so a messenger was dispatched to the Island under a flag of truce, with a list of the general's things to be packed for him. When they arrived, Barton couldn't help smiling. Besides his dress uniform, the fastidious Richard Prescott had sent for a jar of pomatum, a box of talcum powder, several kinds of smelling salts and two large bottles of eau de cologne, bergamont and lavender.

Three days later, General Prescott was taken under guard to Providence, then through Connecticut and into New York, where he was delivered to Washington's headquarters on the Hudson. Sometime later, he was exchanged for the captured American General Charles Lee of Connecticut.

Barton was the hero of the day. "Brave Barton" ballads were composed and sung, and he was wildly applauded wherever he went. A grateful Congress presented him with a vote of thanks and an elegant sword.

In May, 1778, the British made an attack on Warren, Rhode Island, and during the fighting at Bristol Ferry, Barton received a serious wound in his thigh that put him out of the fighting forever; but he continued to serve in other ways. He was appointed customs inspector and elected to the Rhode Island Legislature, and at long last settled down with his family.

However, in 1781, Barton joined forces with Ira Allen (brother of Ethan Allen of "Green Mountain Boy" fame), John Paul Jones and others and petitioned the governor of Vermont for a grant of unsettled land up near the Canadian border. They had intended to call the new township

Providence, but acting on a sudden impulse, Barton, with his ever-ready hunting knife, scratched the name *Providence* from the charter and substituted *Barton*. The papers were passed, and from that day to this, the town has been Barton, Vermont.

In that wild, unbroken wilderness, in the year 1794, William Barton cleared some four or five acres of land, and he cut timber on fifteen acres more. He built a log cabin of one room, with neither floor nor chimney, and lived alone. The next year, he raised thirty to forty bushels of wheat.

Apparently, he got into a lot of controversies. He chopped down some big trees which a neighbor claimed he had no right to. He considered he was being unjustly taxed and stoutly refused to pay a real estate tax on some land he sold to a man named Wadhams. Wadhams, learning that the title was in dispute, repurchased it from another man and demanded that Barton return the money paid him. This Barton refused to do, and after several hearings and court actions and a judgment to pay the original sum plus costs, Barton wrathfully shouted, "I'll never pay it! I'll go to jail and rot there before I'll pay one red cent I don't owe."

And go to jail he did, in Danville . . . *and stayed there for fourteen years!*

His release came about in a most extraordinary and sudden manner. Lafayette, touring the country in 1825, visited Windsor, Vermont, and learning that Colonel William Barton, whom he had known during the war, was "languishing in jail," for nonpayment of what seemed a trivial debt, was horrified.

"How does it happen," the Marquis asked, "that the government which Barton served so bravely and with such honor, is so ungrateful? Why hasn't someone come forward to pay this money and avert such a disgrace?"

Lafayette, much upset, sent a personal draft to General Fletcher of Lyndon, Vermont, covering Barton's indebtedness. And Barton was simply told, one morning, that he was free.

He was furious! He protested; he stormed. He shook his fist and said he would not leave Danville. But they turned him out, and so, because he could no longer "languish in jail," in Vermont, he went back to Rhode Island, and six years later he died, aged eighty-three.

When I first heard this story, I thought it was the most improbable tale ever told about a military hero. But there's an answer to almost everything.

You see, there was no jail in Danville; so Barton was put up at the tavern, where he had comfortable quarters, three square meals a day and was pointed out to guests as a very special "prisoner." He greatly enjoyed being the object of so much attention and didn't want to give it up!

His sentence restricted him to the jail yard, but in his case, the yard was all of Caledonia County. There were beautiful lakes and streams to fish in, and he could hunt whenever it pleased him in that virgin country.

In other words, Colonel Barton, for fourteen years, had been living the life of Riley, at public expense!

II

If there was any one Yankee that the British commander occupying Castine, Maine, in 1780, wanted to get even with, it was General Peleg Wadsworth. He had been aide-de-camp to Artemus Ward at Dorchester Heights, had served with John Sullivan at the battle of Rhode Island and had been second in command of the ill-fated rebel expedition to Castine the year before. Recently, his Yankee troops had seriously interfered with the British marauding parties and "shaving mills"—as the small British vessels were called—which were constantly attacking the coastal towns. So General Campbell had a personal score to settle with Wadsworth.

During that winter, a Maine Tory, Waldo Dicke, approached the English with some welcome news.

"I have just found out where that Yankee general, Wadsworth, is," he said. "He has moved into a little house overlooking the St. George River in Thomaston. He has only a few soldiers around the place at night, and you can take him easily."

In February, 1781, Campbell dispatched Lieutenant Stockton and twenty-five men to go after Wadsworth. They boarded a sloop that Waldo Dicke, the Tory, had stolen, and sailed down the coast from Castine to Thomaston. Anchoring in the Wessaweskeag River, they walked four miles across frozen marshes and fields of crusted

snow to Wadsworth's house. Around midnight they over-
powered the guard and opened fire.

The first volley ripped the front door from its hinges and
set fire to the kitchen. General Wadsworth leaped out of
bed, grabbed his blunderbuss in one hand and a fusee in
the other and fired point-blank at the invaders, wounding
several.

Mrs. Wadsworth ran at once to the room where their
two children were sleeping with a Miss Fenno, and finding
them unharmed, ran back to her husband. Just as she
reached him, a musket ball shattered the general's left
shoulder and he sank to the floor. Outnumbered twenty to
one, his house on fire and himself wounded, Wadsworth
surrendered.

One of Stockton's men helped him dress and wrapped a
blanket around his shoulders. Wadsworth was then pushed
out the back door into deep snow. Bleeding badly and in
great pain, he was made to walk a mile in the subzero
temperature. He was then assisted onto the back of a horse
and rode the remaining three miles to the waiting sloop.

Shoved onto a bunk, General Wadsworth was left to
nurse his wound as best he could, listening to the loud
talk of the soldiers as they passed the rum bottles up on
deck.

When the sloop arrived at Castine, the Tories and British
soldiers crowded the wharf to hiss and taunt the Yankee
general. Cries of "Hang old Wadsworth!" "Let's lynch
him!" were heard, but the prisoner was taken safely into
Fort George and placed under guard in the officers' quar-

ters. British General Campbell sent his personal surgeon to dress Wadsworth's wounded shoulder; he was given a clean suit of clothes and that night was invited to dine with the British staff.

Then he was taken away and locked up.

In due course General Wadsworth applied for parole or exchange, but was refused. Weeks passed slowly. Then one day in spring he heard the tramp of heavy feet and spurred boots coming down the corridor. The door was flung open and a familiar figure burst into the room. "Your fellow prisoner!" said an officer, and Wadsworth looked into the worried face of Major Benjamin Burton.

As soon as he could, without being overheard, Burton whispered, "I've got bad news, sir. Campbell has sent to New York for a ship to take us to England. If we go on trial there, we'll hang sure as God made little apples."

Wadsworth said grimly, "Somehow we've got to get out of here!"

The windows of their room were heavily barred and the floor was solid stone. Only the pine-paneled ceiling looked promising. If they could remove one of the panels, they could climb into the empty room above and get out on the roof. Wadsworth felt they would have no difficulty in lowering themselves to the ground, and with luck they might get across the yard, scale the twenty-foot wall, swim the moat and make a break for the shore a mile away.

Help came unexpectedly from another captured Yankee, Barnabas Cunningham, who was acting as mess attendant in the officers' quarters. Recognizing him, Wadsworth said casually, "I have to mend my boots. Could you find me a gimlet?" Barnabas nodded, and when he fetched supper, among the knives and forks was the gimlet.

As soon as it was dark that night, and for many nights thereafter, Wadsworth stood by the door where he could watch the sentries and block their view of what was going on inside. Burton climbed on a table and with the gimlet bored a series of small holes in the pine panel above their heads. As the sawdust fell, it was quickly collected and burned in the stove.

At every meal, the two Yankees saved small pieces of bread, to which they added soot from the stove, and made pellets with which they plugged the holes to hide them. The job was not quite complete when they overheard their guards talking about a ship which had arrived at Castine that morning. It was going to sail immediately for London!

If two men ever prayed hard, Burton and Wadsworth did! They prayed for a stormy night and good luck. Their prayers were answered by an early-season thunderstorm that was a ring-tailed pealer!

When the first clap of thunder came, Major Burton leaped onto the table, thrust the blade of his knife through the plugged-up holes, worked it back and forth until one end of the panel was loose. Then, as another blast of thunder shook the fortress, he yanked, and down came the panel in a cloud of dust and splinters.

Grabbing Wadsworth's blanket, Burton tossed it up

[15]

through the opening; then he helped the wounded general onto the table, boosted him through the hole in the ceiling and pulled himself up.

Vivid lightning played around Fort George, lighting up every corner and crevice. Suddenly the heavens opened, and the old stone fort was drenched with a torrential downpour that drowned out all sound of the two men's pushing and shoving against an outside door. When it gave way, they landed sprawling on the wind-swept, rain-lashed roof.

They ran to the end of the building where Burton jammed one end of the blanket over a spike and slid quickly to the ground. Wadsworth followed, but just as he landed in Burton's arms a sudden flash of lightning revealed five soldiers running straight toward them. Instantly the officers flattened themselves against the wet jog of the wall and turned away their faces. The guards went right by without seeing them.

Dodging the sentries, the fugitives ran across the parade ground, climbed the outside wall and dropped into the moat. Fortunately, the water was not deep. They waded a short distance and climbed out to scurry through the tall, wet grass of an open field.

Wadsworth reached out a trembling hand and grasped Burton's. "Thank God we made it!" he whispered. "Now . . . we'd better separate. I'll meet you down on the shore. If I'm not there in an hour, wait for me at daybreak on the other side of the cove."

Burton was soon lost in the darkness, and Wadsworth, familiar with the ground from his battle experience there two years before, dodged from tree to stump to bush, badly bruised by brambles and rocks, and his shoulder aching almost unbearably. But he stumbled on, sniffing every few yards for the smell of the ocean. One last brilliant flash of lightning showed him where he was, and minutes later he crept out from the trees onto the beach.

He slumped down against a rock to rest and wait. Burton failed to show up; so the general crawled to the water. It was low tide and the mud was deep and sticky. He waded slowly, up to his armpits, for more than half a mile, across the cove that today bears his name. He was so exhausted when he reached the farther shore that he could barely drag himself under some low-hanging branches, out of sight. As he stretched his weary body on the fragrant ferns, he heard, far off in the distance, the last rumble of thunder as the storm passed out to sea. He drowsed off, only dimly hearing the barking of dogs, shouts and shots, in the distance.

When the warm rising sun touched his face, General Wadsworth awoke, sore and stiff all over. He sat up and looking around, saw the bushes behind him move although there was no wind. He watched, listened, heard a twig snap and then saw Major Burton coming cautiously toward him.

"I've been looking for you," Burton said. "We must leave here at once! They're after us on shore and in boats! I found an Indian canoe back a piece, and we had better take it."

Dawn was just breaking as they launched the canoe and

with swift noiseless strokes shot out from the shadows of the bank. Rounding a bend, they almost ran into a barge that was filled with British soldiers who were hunting them. Bullets whizzed over their heads and the water around them boiled. But with the help of the fast-moving current, they escaped again by the skin of their teeth and crossed the river.

Leaving the canoe, they plunged into the forest. Hiding by day and crawling through the underbrush and woods at night, they traveled for miles, coming out at last at the cabin of an old friend near Lincolnville. He gave them food and urged them to stay, but Wadsworth, fearing they would be seen by Tory spies, refused.

It was nearly three weeks later when the two weary, bearded and nearly starved officers reached safety. Major Burton went at once to his home in Cushing, and General Wadsworth to Thomaston. He found his house empty, his family having removed to Plymouth, Massachusetts, where he joined them.

In 1785 after the Revolutionary War, Peleg Wadsworth moved to Falmouth, now Portland, Maine, where he built the first brick block and used it as his home and general store. Today that same brick building on Congress Street is known as the Wadsworth-Longfellow house.

Sometime around 1800, as a reward for his services, Wadsworth was allowed to purchase 7,800 acres of land between the Saco and Ossipee Rivers for twelve and a half cents an acre, and on that tract of land he founded the town of Hiram, named for the King of Tyre, the First and

Most Excellent Grand Master of Free Masons—Wadsworth was an active member of St. John's Lodge No. 1 of Boston.

The eighteen-room Wadsworth house in Hiram still stands, and in the room where he drilled militia during the war of 1812, you can see the general's desk, books, boots, gun and other things, including a candelabra given him by Lafayette.

General Wadsworth's grandchildren used to love to visit him at Hiram, where they could roam the woods at will. And at the end of the day, perhaps, he would sit in front of his cheerful fireplace telling his grandson the story: "How Major Burton and I escaped from the British at Castine."

His grandson's name was Henry Wadsworth Long-fellow.

General Peleg Wadsworth

Elizabeth Bartlett, his wife

JOEL DUNNE

Every time I hear some feller on one of those confounded quiz programs asking what "switchel" is, I'm reminded of the mess that Joel Dunne got into the day he cut the Widder Riley's marsh grass between Lynn and Saugus, Massachusetts. All this happened many years ago, long before there was any Revere Beach or even a shore road from Boston; in fact it was before the town where shoes were made was called Lynn; it was called Saugust, spelled with a final "t."

The Widder Riley lived in a small thatched cottage up back of the Blue Anchor Tavern, and she was quite a gal— a little on the plump side, fair skinned and a bang-up cook. She was considered a "ketch" for any man, but strangely enough she would have nothing to do with the dandies who hung around the tavern, preferring to pass pleasantries with old "Bow-legs," an itinerant character that the tavern keeper had taken in out of the storm.

His real name was Joel Dunne; he had arrived on a wild November night so weary and chilled he frequently stepped into a bush or lay in the ditch to catch his breath. His enormous shoes, made from uncurried leather, had great holes through which the miry ooze of the marsh squished and splashed. His gray leggings and leather small clothes were besmirched with mud and pitch, and his wide-brimmed rusty brown hat, flaggy and flapping, offered little protection against the driving sleet.

Around Joel's waist was a fox skin belt in which he preserved his personal possessions: an Indian pipe, rusty sheath knife, a coin or two and a handful of soggy acorns tied up in some rags. Every so often, when the going got tough, he would lean heavily on a walking stick and with one bony hand wipe the whiskers out of his eyes. He had a scraggly black beard and long, matted hair. And the wind was blowing a gale.

Night had fallen when old Bow-legs reached the foot of the hill on which the tavern stood in Saugust. As he crept nearer, he made out the rain-lashed, creaking sign and the post where in summer a big, brown bear was chained for the amusement of the guests. At the broad stone steps he collapsed, his forlorn figure outlined by the mellow light from the taproom window slanting through the sleet onto the steps and mud puddles. With one last surge of strength, Bow-legs banged on the door with his cane.

And Cap'n Thomas Marshall was no man to turn away a traveler in trouble. In no time he had Joel in front of the fire and was pouring brandy down his gullet. It took several slugs to bring him to, but after he'd had 'em and a bowl of hot turkey soup and a thick slab of savory roast beef, he was able to sit up, puff on his pipe and talk about his troubles.

He had walked, so he said, all the way from Plymouth, a distance of one hundred miles by the roads of those days.

Cap'n Marshall gave him a blanket and let him sleep in the haymow, and in the morning Joel was fresh as a daisy. He appeared bright and early in the great, warm kitchen of the tavern and asked, "Now what can I do to pay you for my food and night's lodging?"

Somewhat surprised, Cap'n Marshall said, "I dunno. How would you like to chop a little wood?"

Joel straightened up, as well as he could with his badly bowed legs, and said proudly, "I don't wish to boast, sir, but there's not a man in the Bay Colony who can beat me at chopping wood."

After a hearty breakfast, they led him out back to the woodpile, and in two shakes of a lamb's tail, the air was filled with flying chips and chunks of wood. Never had Cap'n Marshall seen anyone chop and split and saw and sing the way that tramp did.

That night he said to Joel, "You know, firewood is mighty important to a tavern like this. If you'd like to stay on and get out some wood for us, you'd be mighty welcome."

So Joel stayed, and his woodpile became the wonder of all who stopped at the Blue Anchor Tavern.

On winter mornings, he'd start at sunup with his saw and ax and gun slung over his shoulder, for the great Lynn woods, and there in the deep, silent, snow-covered forest, he'd work all day, stopping only for a bite of lunch or to take a shot at a rabbit or some partridges. Joel was a good hunter and he brought many a deer, duck and other delicacy to grace the table of Cap'n Marshall's popular tavern.

Some months after his arrival in Saugust, Joel moved his woodpile from the rear of the tavern to a place in plain view of arriving guests. Against the sunny side of a big ledge, he piled driftwood which he hauled from the beach in his little cart, driftwood that would snap and sputter with sparks and blue flames on cold winter nights. Then he laid up a double row of birch logs ten feet high, and back of these was a mighty pile of split wood, stacked neat as a pin, reaching to the eaves of the tavern.

That mountain of wood was a sight to warm the heart of any traveler, and for Widder Riley it held a special fascination. Whenever she went by the tavern and saw Joel a-chopping and a-singing, she'd say to herself, "Faith, and there's a man what's good for something, even if he is bow-legged."

On the q.t. she made him a pair of mittens, and equally on the sly Joel went over and cut her a cord of wood. And then one hot summer day when Joel was passing her cottage, the Widder asked him in and inquired if he'd like to cut the grass on her land down by the shore.

Bow-legs allowed as how, "There ain't nothin' I'd ruther do on a hot day than cut and stack grass on the marsh," so Mrs. Riley packed him a nice lunch of cold chicken, a couple of boiled eggs, a piece of poor man's pie—and she also mixed him a jug of switchel.

"It'll keep you from sweating," she said.

Joel went to the tavern to get his tools, leaving his basket and jug alongside the stoop, where some of the servants, jealous of Joel and his woodpile and the Widder, found it. They spread the chicken with mustard fresh from the Slade mill up in Chelsea, tucked red peppers into the eggs and into Joel's jug they poured a pint of Old Medford rum.

Busy with the business of packing his cart with rope and boards, scythe and rake, Bow-legs paid no attention till one of the pranksters said, "Better be careful and not get sun struck, Joel; it's powerful hot on the marsh today."

Another lout continued, "Yeah, I heered 'bout a feller over to Salem what sweat so much he . . . dissolved! Honest Injun! All they found of him was the buttons offen his coat in a weeny puddle of salt water."

Joel went about his business without answering. The particular piece of marsh that Widder Riley owned was where the General Electric plant stands today. The tide was out, and Joel was soon swinging his scythe and tying up armfuls of the fragrant grass to form the foundation of a staddle. Then he skillfully added layer after layer, and in a few hours he had a round, fat haystack higher than his head.

Suddenly his stomach told him 'twas lunchtime, so he climbed up on the stack and plopped an egg into his mouth. The poor feller darn near choked, but he washed it down with several quick swallows of switchel, which had, he thought, a strange but not unwelcome flavor. Each bite of food that he took was hotter than the one before, so naturally he had to drink more switchel, and before he realized it, he was so drowsy he couldn't sit up.

Slowly his head fell forward, and in a trice he was fast asleep. During that hot afternoon while the summer sun beat down on Bow-legs, an unusually high tide crept in over the marsh, but Joel didn't awaken. Finally the sun went down behind the Saugust hills and a cold, wet fog rolled in from the sea. It was pitch dark when Joel came to.

He didn't remember who he was or where he was; his head ached something terrible and his tongue tasted like a feather bed afire, and—he was soaking wet all over!

"Gor-blimy, I must be dissolving!" he thought, and reaching down to feel of his feet which had both gone to sleep and were numb as logs, his hand struck water.

Scared almost out of his wits now, Joel put his trembling fingers to his lips and tasted. "*Salt!*" he screamed. "*I am dissolving!*"

At that moment he heard men's voices, out of the fog, and someone shouted, "Shut up, you fool and climb into the boat!"

The boys from the tavern had come to his rescue, feeling it would spoil their fun if they let Joel drown.

Bow-legs could tell by the way he felt there had been something in the Widder Riley's jug besides switchel— something besides just water, molasses, ginger and vinegar— and whenever he saw her after that, he would just grunt and turn his back. He never touched another drop of hard liquor. Oh, he would take a mug of ale now and then or a little wine, but the sight of a rum barrel made him shiver; especially he shivered when several barrels at a time arrived from Barbados to be stored in the cellar of the Blue Anchor Tavern, for Cap'n Marshall kept a good supply of liquor on hand for his thirsty trade.

Hearing that the Ancient & Honorable Artillery Company was marching to Lynn for a grand celebration, the genial host invited them to stop for refreshments at the Blue Anchor, and ordered a special hogshead of Old Medford to use in their punch. It took a pair of oxen all day to drag the cask, gaily decorated with ribbons and red, white and blue rosettes, over the dusty winding roads to Saugust, where it arrived just as Joel was finishing his chores and, amid loud huzzas, was drawn up the hill and placed just east of the tavern. The wheels were chocked and the oxen turned loose, and everyone but Joel went to make merry in the taproom. He began to worry about the harm all that rum might do on the morrow.

Hours later he was still worrying about it. "Supposin'," he said to himself, "those Ancient and Honorable gentlemen have never tasted rum. They might take too much as I did and have the horrors. That would be awful! I'd better go see if it's still there."

When he saw the hogshead looming up big as a barn against the starlit sky, Joel was suddenly taken with a desire to protect his fellow men. He grabbed a crowbar, pried out the chocks, gave the wheels a gentle push and jumped out of the way.

But being bow-legged, he didn't jump far and fast

enough; his foot caught in one of the wheels and he was whirled round and round, down, down the hill, where the dray smashed against a rock, and with a crash the hogshead split wide open.

When rescuers came with torches and lanterns—and cups and pails and straws—they found poor Bow-legs lying face down in a puddle of rum. He had given his life in a cause that he believed was just.

CAPTAINS
AND CANNIBALS

T HE most exclusive men's club in America was organized in the summer of 1779 at Salem, Massachusetts. Its members were Yankee shipmasters and supercargoes who had navigated the stormy seas around and beyond the Cape of Good Hope at the southern extremity of Africa, or Cape Horn at the lowest point of South America. The records of their voyages, and the objects they brought back from the far corners of the earth, are preserved in the Peabody Museum of Salem.

Membership was definitely limited. It didn't matter how many times a Gloucester or Cape Cod captain had braved the fog and ice on the Grand Banks, nor how many times a Maine or Nantucket skipper had "crossed the Pond." If he hadn't been "round the Capes," he wasn't eligible to join the East India Marine Society.

The young men who founded this society opened the way to the riches of the Orient. Elias Hasket Derby, the famous Salem merchant, sent his ex-privateer *Grand Turk* to Cape Town in 1784, and there Captain Jonathan Ingersoll bought tea and other oriental goods which sold like hot cakes in Salem. As a result, Derby sent the *Grand Turk* on a second voyage to the East, and she pushed through to Canton—the first New England vessel to enter a Chinese port.

Visitors to the Peabody Museum always exclaim at the enormous Chinese Lowestoft punch bowl bearing a sketch of the *Grand Turk* which can be seen in the center of East India Marine Hall beside the pair of remarkable Chinese porcelain soup tureens in the form of geese. These are twenty-two inches long, fourteen inches wide and twenty-one inches high—"visible reminders of the splendid dinners which, preceded by processions through the streets of Salem, marked the annual meetings of the East India Marine Society during the first dozen years of its existence." (Walter M. Whitehill: *The East India Marine Society and the Peabody Museum of Salem. A Sesquicentennial History.*)

Captain Jonathan Carnes landed the first consignment of pepper, from Sumatra, and Captain Jacob Crowninshield brought the first elephant from India on the *America*.

I thought this last would make fine material for a Yankee Yarns broadcast, but the clips I had from newspapers and magazines disagreed on dates and details. Even different names were given. In desperation I appealed to the Peabody Museum of Salem to straighten me out.

Librarian Charles H. P. Copeland heard me through and

then said with a smile, "I don't wonder you are mixed up. There were two early elephants both called Old Bet, four different ships named *America* and there were five Captains Crowninshield, all brothers. But here is the original log book of the right *America*."

He pointed to the date of October 25, 1795, and I read: "*Calcutta to America. Took aboard some punkins and greens for the elephant.*" And printed underneath was "*Elephant on Board*" in the bold hand of Nathaniel Hathorne, father of the famous New England author who, incidentally, added a W in his last name.

Charles Copeland led me into another room to see the portraits of Jacob and Benjamin Crowninshield, owners of the *America*, but when I saw the remarkable collection of oil portraits of Billy Gray, Elias Hasket Derby, Nathaniel Bowditch and Captain William Driver, I forgot all about elephants. William Driver was mate of the ship *Clay* when she made her memorable voyage to the Fiji Islands after bêche-de-mer.

The bêche-de-mer is a sea worm, usually about eight inches long and roughly three inches thick. It is dark brown in color and its tough skin is covered with slime. Hundreds of natives were employed to pick these loathsome sluglike creatures (which spewed out their guts when handled) off the coral reefs and carry them to nearby pools where they were washed in salt water. Then they were boiled for nearly an hour in big black kettles and spread to dry. Packed in matting bags and stowed aboard ship, they were carried to the Orient where they commanded high prices as a food delicacy for Chinese mandarins who used the bêche-de-mer to flavor their delectable, gelatinous soups and as an aphrodisiac.

Native Fijians were glad to wade in the surf and scoop up the slimy slugs in great quantities for the trinkets offered by the Salem captains and especially for anything made of metal, as their tools were made of shell. A chisel, for instance, fashioned by the ship's blacksmith from an old iron hoop and attached to a wooden handle was worth a whole day's labor, and any kind of musket or firing piece would buy a native's labor for a month.

The Fiji Island trade became practically a monopoly for Salem captains. Sometimes, a half-dozen Salem ships would be in the Fijis at the same time, and when they returned home after having disposed of the bêche-de-mer in China and taken on a cargo of spices, silk, tea and various treasures, their profit was considerable.

When Captain Benjamin Vanderford in the *Clay* transported the first cargo of bêche-de-mer ever carried by a white man, he left his mate, William Driver, in the Fijis among the cannibals to supervise the gathering and curing of a second cargo.

Opening an exhibition case, Charles Copeland removed a porringer. "This," he explained, "was made from the pump box of H.M.S. *Bounty*. It was given to Captain William Driver in appreciation of his returning sixty-four of the *Bounty's* crew from Tahiti to Pitcairn Island."

I knew, of course, about the mutiny on the *Bounty* and Captain Bligh, and dimly I remembered something about

Captain Driver and the American flag. Copeland quickly launched into that story.

On a wintry morning in 1831, the brig *Charles Doggett* lay at the wharf in Salem, trim and ready for a voyage around the world. Captain William Driver stood on deck with a group of friends who had come to wish him Godspeed, when one of them handed him a flag folded into a triangle. As the banner was run to the masthead, Captain Driver stepped forward and said with deep emotion, "To the finest flag of them all! Let me call thee Old Glory!" That was the first time the Stars and Stripes was ever hailed as Old Glory.

Years later, when Captain Driver retired from the sea and went to live in Nashville, Tennessee, he took the old flag with him, and every Washington's Birthday and Fourth of July the flag was unfurled and hung in front of his house. But at the outbreak of the Civil War, being a strong Union man he was worried for fear the southern soldiers might take his Old Glory and destroy it; so he neatly sewed it inside his bed comforter. The Confederates did search his house, but failed to find the flag.

Then, on February 25, 1862, the victorious Northern troops captured Nashville, hauled down the Confederate colors and were about to run up the Stars and Stripes. Out of the crowd stepped Captain William Driver. Saluting, he said, "Wouldn't you like to have my Old Glory?" And a few minutes later the beautiful bunting presented to him in Salem harbor was raised against the southern sky.

Today that flag is on display in the National Museum at
Washington.

Close by the portrait of Captain Driver in the Peabody
Museum I noticed the clear-cut features of another ship-
master, Captain John Henry Eagleston, who carried many
Yankee prospectors "round the Horn" to California in
1849 and brought back to Salem the first lumps and nuggets
of gold of those exciting days. Charlie Copeland tells
me that Captain Eagleston sent some of that early gold to
France and had a magnificent case made for a pocket watch.
It is decorated with a wreath of roses, the petals being
formed out of various kinds of gold of different colors.

Captain Eagleston also made numerous voyages to the
Fiji Islands and had many exciting adventures with the
cannibals there. It was he who brought to Salem, among
other things, war clubs, a wig and a tooth that once belonged to Thakombau, King of the Cannibal Isles.

Seeing that tooth—a huge, irregular molar mounted on a
small block of wood and stained with age—I was reminded
of a story I had heard years before when I lectured at a
meeting of the New Bedford Mariners' Club, held in those
days in the spacious sail loft of Pierce & Kilburn's Ship
Yard in Fairhaven. The customary banquet consisted of
punch, fish chowder, pilot bread, doughnuts, pickles,
cheese and coffee. Sea captains, retired whalers, yachts-
men, artists, writers, coast guard men and rum-runners
gathered to have a darn good time. They might be mortal
enemies at three o'clock in the afternoon, but at seven that
night they were jolly good fellows. I well recall the night

that somebody from the Coast Guard was relating the difficulty he was having in installing a new high-powered engine for his Coast Guard boat. The man next to him said, "Well, if you need any additional help, I will be glad to send the boys over and give you a hand." But the Coast Guard officer shook his head; and I learned that the unshaven chap who offered to help was a leading rumrunner whom the Coast Guard had been chasing for a week!

I don't recall how we got started on cannibals at that particular meeting, but I made a few notes, and here briefly is the story.

Somewhere in the 1830's a captain from Salem was wrecked in the Fiji Islands. He was captured by some fierce-looking natives and tied to a palm tree. From the way they jabbered and danced around him and pointed to a big black kettle sitting on some rocks, he figured they were getting ready for a special feast and that he was going to be the main course.

Just then he saw an enormous black man, naked as the day he was born except for a pair of women's pink corsets, come tearing down the beach like a mad dog. He waved a stout war club, gazed hungrily at the Salem man, then grabbed hold of his own jaw, which was swollen way out, and gave a yell that could be heard for miles. He clutched his black whiskers, yanked at his hair and kicked his big, bare toes into the sand, yelling louder all the time.

The Salem captain asked who this wild man was and was told to his surprise that he was king of all the Fijis and the most ferocious cannibal that ever lived. He had already eaten 500 men, women and children.

"He's mad because the tribe is going to have a good meal offen you and his tooth is so sore he can't chew on your bones," the Fiji native told the white man.

The captain said excitedly, "Tell your king I can stop his pain, but he must do exactly as I say. And if I do stop his toothache, he must agree to let me go. If I fail, the banquet may proceed."

The king agreed. He opened his big jaw and kept pointing to the aching tooth. Six stalwart natives were chosen to supervise the treatment, and the whole village turned out to watch. The captain sent for his medicine kit, which had been saved from the wreck, and took out a bottle of laudanum. He poured about thirty drops into an empty coconut shell and asked several of the natives to contribute their cuds of chewing tobacco. It was an awful-looking mess, but when spiked with brandy, didn't taste so bad. The king downed the whole shellful in one gulp, sank to his knees and went out like a light. The six men stretched him out and straddled his enormous, well-oiled form, holding his arms and legs just in case he came to.

The Salem captain then reached into his medicine chest for the big steel key which he always carried in case he had to make an extraction. This was an innocent-looking device like a miniature cant-dog or woodsman's peavy, with a floating hook. He forced open the cannibal's mouth and shoved in the toe of his own boot to keep it open. He got a good grip on the tooth and as the grinning natives bore down hard, the captain jumped up and backward, twisting and turning the key contraption as he went. The tooth was torn away and came out. Some more brandy was poured down the king's gullet and he slept the rest of the day and that night.

In the morning, his jaw was still sore, but the pain was all gone. The king was so thankful he let the Salem man go free and offered him the ugliest of his thirty-five wives. The skipper didn't fancy the "beauty," and asked for the tooth instead, as a souvenir. And when he got home, he gave it to some museum.

Charles Copeland hadn't heard this version, and neither had Ernest S. Dodge, Director of Peabody Museum, but they assured me that in their collection of Fijian relics there were spears, war clubs, a cannibal's fork, palm leaf fan and wooden pillow, several genuine cannibal wigs and a tooth—presented by Captain John Eagleston—that was yanked from the aching jaw of King Thakombau, the most cruel cannibal that ever lived.

We adjourned to the second floor where the Fijian collection is on display in East Hall. Mr. Dodge picked out one of Thakombau's favorite wigs, a huge headdress of bushy, black hair intricately woven around a bowl-shaped, basket-like frame, and much too large for any human head I ever saw. There was another cannibal wig of a decidedly lighter color. So I asked, "Why is this wig reddish-brown instead of black?"

"The Fijians were very particular about their hair," Ernest Dodge explained. "They spent many hours training it to grow thick and bushy, and some of them dyed their raven locks different colors. First they had to bleach their hair with a solution of lime water made by burning coral and sea shells. They used the leaves of the tumeric tree, a plant like ginger, to produce a strong yellow dye. You can imagine the result!"

"How did they manage to make their hair stand up and be so fuzzy?"

"With the young people, it was careful hair-dressing. On the older folks it was a case of expert wig-making. If a cannibal had thin hair or became bald, he would have a wig made, usually with human hair pulled from the scalps of his victims."

Since the days of the Salem captains, the Fijians have turned to more modern methods. They bleach their raven hair with strong solutions of peroxide, then color it with commercial dyes, preferring the brilliant shades of henna, yellow and flaming orange.

I reached for one of the war clubs—the most brutal-looking object I ever hefted. It is elaborately carved to a sharp point and beautifully balanced. Thakombau had killed a lot of his enemies with that, often just for the fun of it. If people disagreed with him . . . *wham;* they were on their way to the dinner table. He killed his first victim, a boy of his own age, when he was eight. This was considered fine training for a future warrior. It is re-corded that before he reformed and became a Christian, Thakombau killed at least 800 men, women and children and ate his share of them.

Ernest Dodge picked up a native Fijian fork, whittled out of black palm. Some of the cannibal chieftains believed that after eating human flesh a sort of florescence remained on their hands; so Thakombau had used this identical wooden fork so his hands wouldn't glow in the dark, and the missionaries and white traders wouldn't know that he had been eating "long pig."

I mentioned the big black kettles with a missionary about to be boiled, so frequently seen in cartoons. Dodge laughed. "That was a popular idea, but the cannibals never had kettles unless some trader left behind his bêche-de-mer kettle or they got hold of a whaler's try-pot from a wreck. They may have boiled a few of their victims, but mostly they were roasted in an oven made by digging a pit and lining it with stones. Anyway, the Fijians seldom ate white folks—they said the flavor was too strong. They preferred other Fijians, their enemies. And because they were afraid of the white man's guns, they almost never killed a sea captain or a missionary."

Thakombau had thirty-five wives to wait on him, and he kept a club for each wife. The wives were constantly in fear that he would die in battle, because they would have to die too. It was the custom when a chieftain died to strangle all his wives so they could accompany him to the spirit world. Every wife knew this and accepted it as part of her religion. It was the honor and privilege of the eldest son, when his father died, to pull the ceremonial death cord affixed to the neck of his mother. When his own father, Tanoa, was dying, Thakombau promised him that the ancient custom would be speedily carried out, and as soon as Tanoa had breathed his last, Thakombau, as was his right, tightened the cord around his mother's neck and choked her to death. Three more wives were slain before missionaries broke in and put a stop to the proceedings.

For years, missionaries, British and United States government officials and all the Yankee ship captains tried to get the Fijians to give up cannibalism, and after a long time they succeeded. On October 30, 1853, Thakombau finally gave Reverend Joseph Waterhouse permission to move into the capital village of Mbau and establish a mission. Then on April 27, 1854, he told the Reverend Mr. Waterhouse that he had decided to become a Christian. He took the biblical name of Ebenezer, and 300 of his subjects hit the "sawdust trail" with him.

Thakombau's power as a chief had been weakening, but now that he was a Christian, his fortunes looked brighter. The United States gave him a shipload of much-needed guns and ammunition, and King George Tubou of nearby Tonga supplied the new convert with several thousand warriors and war canoes. Together they defeated what few rebellious subjects remained, and the villainous cannibal was now established as the enlightened King of the Fiji Isles.

But his new estate was more expensive than he knew how to handle, and he sold out to the British. On October 10, 1874, the Fiji Islands, some 250 in number, became a British Crown Colony. Thakombau was allotted an annual pension of £1500, and he presented his best war club to Queen Victoria as a symbol of her authority over the islands. When the club was found in Windsor Castle in 1931, it was given back to the Fijians.

Thakombau died in 1883, a serene, respected elder statesman, but when the Salem captains knew him, he was the wickedest and cruelest cannibal the world has ever known.

UNEXPECTED FINDS

Every time I hear of some strange object's being found up attic or down cellar or dug from somebody's back yard, I can't sit still until I have seen it, made a few photographs and asked a lot of questions. Usually these things don't amount to a hill of beans, but once in a while something shows up worth telling about, like the so-called "Indian relic" now in the basement of the Peabody Museum of Salem.

Back in 1810 or thereabouts, workmen digging a cellar for a house being built for Thomas Marshall Burnham in the village of Essex, Massachusetts, came upon a large, oval-shaped stone firmly embedded in the sand. As they pried it loose, one man exclaimed, "Hey! Look at the face on that there rock!" And sure enough, there was a smooth-shaven face with deep-set eyes, unmistakably Roman nose and small, well-shaped ears.

The head, which had been chiseled from a piece of granite, was bigger than life-size and of course attracted considerable attention. Most of the villagers said at once,

"Indians did it!" But teachers from a nearby school shook their heads. "He's a Roman statesman! Must have come from Europe!"

Thomas Burnham didn't know what they'd found, but he dragged it to his barn, and when the new house was finished and the lawn graded and fenced in, he had the crudely sculptured head hoisted onto the stout pine post of his gateway. Somebody suggested it would look more lifelike if it was "dickied up a bit" so Burnham got out his paint pots and brushes and gave the mysterious stone a pink bald pate, red lips and bright blue eyes. Folks came from as far away as Boston to gaze and wonder what the thing was and where in Tophet it had come from.

There on the main street of Essex, Old Baldy remained through all the icy blasts of winter and summer's sizzling sun. Small boys would have liked to move him around but he was far too big and heavy; so they frequently tied a colored scarf under his chin and put various styles of headgear on his granite dome. One very special hat, a receptacle, was reserved for the night before the Fourth of July.

In 1825 Burnham moved his family to Boston, where he started what is said to be the first second-hand bookshop in the city. Although this was a new and decidedly different enterprise, in just a few years it occupied two buildings of four stories each, every shelf sagging with books of all kinds and thousands of pamphlets and periodicals.

Naturally this bookshop became the meeting place for

authors, antiquarians and other men of learning, and as Thomas had had his stone hauled over from Essex and placed in the front window, some of the conversation revolved around it. By this time most of the lurid paint had chipped off or was respectably faded and Old Nero looked quite dignified.

A young competitor whose store was a few doors down Washington Street from Cornhill actually believed that it was the strange image which brought Burnham so much business, and in a tactful way he let it be known that if Burnham would sell, at a reasonable price, he would buy. Burnham, now wealthy and known as "The Squire of Chebacco Parish," at first refused flatly to sell his good luck relic, but on being offered $200, he gave in. The stony eyes gazed out of another window, and the head continued to attract attention although it never brought its new owner the business that Thomas Burnham enjoyed.

There was one foreign-looking gentleman who would stand for minutes at a time scrutinizing the granite image. One day he entered the shop accompanied by a friend and politely asked, "Where did that piece of sculpture come from?"

The owner, noting their keen interest and their Danish accents, was quick to tell what he knew. The stone, he explained, had been excavated in historic Essex, the home port of many sailing vessels, and probably, because of its weight, had been picked up by some Yankee skipper on the shore of Greece or Spain or Italy and heaved into the hold as ballast. Then he added for good measure, "We don't know which of the Old Masters executed this fine example of Roman sculpture as it was done so many thousands of years ago. Of course it isn't as important here in Boston as it would be in, say, London or Paris."

The two men argued and gestured and finally plunked down some money. That night the mysterious stone was carefully wrapped in burlap, packed in straw, crated and carted to a sturdy sailing vessel bound for Denmark.

Several months later there appeared in Copenhagen newspapers a glowing account of the rare example of early Roman sculpture recently purchased by the National Museum and drawing crowds there every day. Eventually among the visitors was a tart old skipper from Chebacco Parish back in Massachusetts. He had intended to look at the models of whale boats, but casually joining a group of students, he turned a corner and there, bigger than life and twice as natural, was the old "Indian relic" of his boyhood days.

"Blow me down! If it ain't my old friend Baldy from Tom Burnham's fence post. What in thunder are you doing way over here?"

Old Baldy didn't say anything, but the museum officials did. They took the cantankerous captain aside and got the whole story. When they had checked with the town fathers of Essex, Massachusetts, U. S. A., and were convinced they had been victims of a shrewd Yankee deal, they dumped the stone into a hogshead and shipped it back to America. It was unloaded at a wharf in Salem, but when I started to look for it, nobody knew what had become of it.

George S. McIntyre of Essex, who brought this story to my attention, said he understood the head was in Peabody Museum. There I hastened with camera and flash outfit to see what the controversial head looks like today. But it was gone! Not a trace of the old Roman could we find; so we drove to Essex and spent two whole days calling on various people who might help us. The image had been for a spell at the Essex Historical society, but a careful search through all the cupboards and closets failed. I finally called on a Mrs. Goodhue, who telephoned Robert Smallage. Mr. Smallage drove us out into the country to call on Reverend Warren Francis Lowe. He insisted the head was in Peabody Museum. So back we went, and lo and behold! there it was! It had been stored in a far, dark corner of the basement and completely forgotten.

The stolid, grim-looking face bears a striking resemblance to Mussolini. Although referred to by some historians as an Indian relic, it definitely is not. Maybe it was chiseled by some local man living on the shore of the Essex River. Or maybe it really was brought from Europe as ballast by some long-forgotten skipper. In either case, it had quite a career.

II

The Essex stone head is a bulky object, measuring fourteen inches from the chin up. But small things too have been saved for years simply because they caused someone a bit of curiosity. Mrs. Watson, of Saugus, Massachusetts, telephoned me one day to say that she had "something oriental" that she believed was bad luck. "It may even have a curse on it! Will you come over and tell me what you think it is?"

We found the lady all in a dither. She invited us to sit down and immediately launched into this story.

Around 1920, Mr. Watson was working on a construction job at East Boston, and every Saturday morning he went aboard some barges to see that the pumps were working. One Saturday his little girl, who was then six or seven, begged to go with him, and being an indulgent father he took her along. She climbed aboard the barge and played around the deck and after a while she cautiously stepped into what was called the "captain's office"—a small cabin filled with papers, tools and old blueprints.

Her eagle eye spotted a small raffia-covered box which lay on the floor in a corner, and when she rejoined her father she was playing with it, opening and shutting the padded, plush-covered top and running her hands over the outside. As it was just an old-fashioned sewing box with a pincushion lid and apparently had been aimed for the wastebasket, he told her she might keep it and take it home.

Along with other souvenirs, the raffia box lay around for years. Then one day in 1945 when Mrs. Watson was cleaning house and sorting out things to throw away, she gave the old pincushion a more careful look. Under the dust and grime was a row of evenly shaped mother-of-pearl shells neatly sewed around the edge. They seemed worth saving so she snipped them off, letting them fall into her family button box.

One shell stuck on tighter than the others, and when finally pried loose revealed a wad of tightly folded tin foil underneath. "Now why would anyone wedge that in there?" she said, noticing at the same time a dark brown stain where glue had been used to hold the wad in place.

Her daughter, now grown up and married, said, "Let's open it up, Mother. Maybe there's something inside!" And grabbing the little wad, she slowly pulled it apart.

Out rolled a semitransparent pink stone with white flecks. After puzzling over this unexpected find, they called in a neighbor who owned a microscope, and all hands took turns peeking through the eyepiece at this strange, lustrous, out-of-shape, squarish stone. Suddenly one of the group shouted, "Here, look at this!"

And as each person leaned over to gaze through the microscope, he saw in the middle of the stone a tiny oriental face, and beside it a clearly defined dagger with a drop of blood on the pointed tip!

Everyone was perplexed, and Mrs. Watson was scared. She had read yarns about Chinese mysteries and tongs and oriental curses; she felt sure the stone would bring bad luck, and she didn't want the accursed thing in her house. Yet she was so curious that she kept it. Every time she saw the little pink lump she had a cold chill, and it was her daughter who had to fetch it for me to look at. As she dropped it in my palm, she gasped, "It's shrinking!"

And Mrs. Watson said in a high, frightened voice, "It's only half as big as it was! Take it out of here!"

Well, we brought the thing home and examined it carefully, but could make nothing out of it. So we took it to a laboratory in Cambridge and watched a scientist—who asked me not to mention his name—poke and scrape and peer, then put a few scrapings in acid. Finally he smiled.

"Unquestionably this is one of the earliest pieces of plastic. It was originally molded, not cut; there are air bubbles all through it."

"What about the oriental face and the dagger those women thought they saw?" I asked.

The professor lifted his eyebrows and looked at me as if I were a small child. "Merely coincidence. Just a poor grade of plastic with flaws in it. It was left in a warm place so the shape changed. It might have resembled an apple or flower or anything. The spots have worn off, but this is certainly a die."

I'm sorry this did not develop into a real oriental mystery —but it's a puzzler none the less. Why in the world did somebody wrap one of a pair of dice in tin foil and then glue it under a mother-of-pearl shell on a pincushion? And who carried such a fancy article aboard a barge at East Boston?

III

Of all the strange objects that have been found in New England, none is more puzzling than the "mystery stone" discovered while workmen were digging a ditch near the shore of Lake Winnipesaukee in 1872. They were about three feet down in the ordinary clay soil peculiar to that vicinity when Seneca Ladd, cashier of a Concord, New Hampshire bank, and collector of Indian relics, came by. He happened to notice an odd-looking lump of earth and picked it up—an irregular ovoid about eight inches in length.

When he tapped it with a stick some of the outer covering dropped off, but a harder incrustation remained, concealing a heavy object underneath. Ladd took his find home and washed it under the pump. To his intense surprise, the clay softened and washed away, leaving a smooth, greenish-black, egg-shaped stone decorated with finely cut designs.

It measured about four inches high and weighed just eighteen ounces. Running through the center of the stone was a perpendicular hole, big as a pencil at the base but tapering to the size of a pencil lead at the top. How that tapering hole was bored or drilled in the stone still remains a mystery.

On the sides were ten different designs, etched or carved with workmanship far superior to that found on aboriginal relics. A small circle, supposedly representing the sun or moon, was as perfect as though struck by a compass. There was also a delicate spiral and a perfect, eight-pointed star. Four arrows or spears were crossed to form the letter "M." There was a three-sided Indian tepee and a beautifully etched ear of corn with seventeen kernels to the row, and in a circle below the corn were what appeared to be a bird in flight, a deer's leg and a bear's paw.

Most surprising of all, occupying one whole side was a human face, definitely not Indian. The features, with closed eyes, broad, flat nose, and thick lips, were more like those of an Aztec, Eskimo or possibly a Polynesian.

After Seneca Ladd's death, the stone was purchased by D. W. Coe, a wealthy resident of Center Harbor, and finally his widow turned it over to the New Hampshire Historical Society where it created countrywide attention. It was first described to me by Kenneth Roberts, the great historical novelist, and at his suggestion I went to Concord. The curator of the Historical Museum, Elmer Hunt, opened a big vault and took out a tin can and carefully uncovered the curious stone. I photographed it from every angle, both in kodachrome and with my movie camera, then I asked, "What is it—some kind of banner stone?"

Hunt said frankly, "We don't know. Why not ask the Smithsonian Institution? They examined it thoroughly over fifty years ago."

So I wrote the Smithsonian, and received, in part, this answer:

SMITHSONIAN INSTITUTION

BUREAU OF AMERICAN ETHNOLOGY

WASHINGTON 25, D. C.

October 29, 1947

Dear Mr. Blackington:

With reference to the carved stone mentioned in your letter, I doubt very much if the face was intended to portray an Indian.

I am convinced the stone was not carved by an Indian, but by some white man who wanted it to appear like Indian art work.

None of the objects resemble in any way the handiwork of Eastern Indians. They never depicted ears of corn or tepees, as those were restricted to the tribes of the West and Southwest.

You are probably aware that in the last century a flourishing business of making fake antiquities was in progress and many a fraudulent artifact found its way into reputable museum collections.

Very truly yours,
Henry B. Collins, Jr.

Well, that's their opinion, and it may be the answer— but that explanation doesn't satisfy me nor a lot of other New Englanders.

Remember, this stone was discovered three feet down in hard-packed clay, going on ninety years ago. The designs are so expertly executed they compare favorably with those of a Tiffany craftsman. Now who, I ask, would take the time to do all that intricate carving on a perfectly smooth egg-shaped stone, and bore a tapering hole through its center? Some college student? Or some eccentric old-time scientist? And, having made such a wondrous conversation piece, would he choose a wild and untraveled region of New Hampshire countryside, to bury his masterpiece in the absurd hope that it would be discovered and thought to be Indian?

IV

Quite often I start out to get one story and suddenly it leads to another far more interesting than the first. And that's what happened when Larry Brown and I drove to Center Harbor, New Hampshire, to see Frederick Sumner Coe, nephew of the man who had once owned the "mystery stone." I had hoped that he might know something about it, but he didn't. As we started to leave, he said as an afterthought, "How'd you like to see the emerald I dug up just five miles from where that stone was found?"

"A real emerald? How big? And what's its value?" I asked incredulously.

Fred Coe grinned. "Well, if it is an emerald, it's the biggest anyone round here ever saw, and should be worth—twenty-five thousand dollars! If you care to drive up to the old Coe mansion, I'll show it to you."

As we drove from Red Hill back to the village, he gave us this story: "Some years ago, I was digging a well on the E. B. Dane estate, and my shovel struck what I thought was a rock. Digging around, I saw it was a magnificent glistening green jewel buried there in the field. I got it out, put it on the scales, and found it weighed approximately four pounds. It was the biggest hunk of green something I had ever seen, and clear as crystal."

We drove into the yard of the Coe mansion and entered a side door. Mr. Coe disappeared and we went into the front parlor to examine the murals—landscape wall paper imported from Alsace-Lorraine, depicting scenes of the

Nile and Italy. You can find a picture of that famous paper following page 76 in the New Hampshire volume of the American Guide Series. We were amazed to see that the original window drapes and rich carpets had withstood the years so well, and when Coe came back he said, "That is because we have kept the shutters closed." He pointed to the antique furniture and said, "That fancy love seat, table, and chair haven't been moved since the day that President Franklin Pierce and John Greenleaf Whittier, the poet, came to call on my uncle."

We followed Fred Coe to the spacious kitchen where he placed a bundle big as a man's head on the table. Unrolling the cloth covering, he displayed the gleaming chunk of "green something," and Larry Brown exclaimed, "If that's an emerald, it's worth a lot more than twenty-five thousand!"

"I suppose it's glass," Coe said, rubbing his chin, "but there's nothing like it around here, and I'd like to find out for sure!"

Now it happened that Larry and I were headed for Severance Lodge in Center Lovell, Maine, only a few miles from Norway where Maine's best-known gem hunter lived—George Robley Howe. I offered to take the green crystal to "Uncle" George, and Fred Coe lugged it out and tossed it on the back seat of our car.

"If it's an emerald," he said with a chuckle, "call me on the phone. If it ain't, just ship it back by express."

It rained most of the way but the sky began to lighten as we crossed into Maine, and as we started the long, steep climb up Pike's Hill, Norway, we could dimly see the red tiled roof of Summit Study, the sturdy two-story home Uncle George had built with his own hands back in 1915. Flanked by graceful golden willows and locust trees, it looked like a castle in the drifting clouds.

I remembered that there was no front door, so we followed the flagstone path around to the side and ducked under a canopy of dripping vines. The living-room door was wide open and we could hear the resonant voice of the aged naturalist as he explained the wonders of Mother Nature to a group of boys from a camp over in Harrison.

"Everything you see in this room, boys, I collected myself. I began collecting birds' eggs, bugs, and butterflies when I was seven years old. I used to bring home caterpillars and keep 'em in my grandfather's straw hat, till he found them."

We squeezed in quietly, hardly noticed by the campers who were sprawled on the floor in front of the fireplace. Uncle George moved over to a big rack.

"These shelves are filled with specimens of rock and minerals I've picked up in the last half century. And these here are semiprecious gems. Remember, there are more jewels right here in Maine than anywhere else. All you have to do is look, and then dig for them."

Suddenly he spied us, gave a quick nod of recognition, but kept on talking. "Here," he said, holding up a chip of smoky quartz, "is one of my earliest discoveries. I found this over in the Bumpus mine. I gave a piece to Vivian

Akers, the photographer; he had a fine lens made of it and still uses it on his camera."

He grabbed another specimen. "And this is something you don't see very often: a rock with lithium in it. That's the lightest metal known, so light, in fact, it will float on water. Good use of this will be made in the aircraft industry if they can get enough of it."

A youngster piped up, "Have you ever found any gold, Mr. Howe?"

"Of course. Many times. Not an awful lot, but enough to make a brooch. You can see people most any day in the summer panning for gold along the Swift River up above Byron. Mr. Skillings, who lives up there, has been prospecting for many years, and has made a living out of it. I found my best nuggets wedged between the roots of goldenrod on the river bank.

"Well, boys, I guess that's about all for today. When you come back Friday, I'll show you my garnets, jaspers, and tourmalines, and if you want to, we can go over to South Paris. Lots of semiprecious stones over there.

"Don't forget to sign the guest book before you go. I have more than four thousand callers a year, and there are about one hundred forty-nine thousand names in that book."

The boys got up, applauded and drifted out reluctantly. Uncle George came out from behind the rack of minerals and shook hands. His hair and neatly trimmed beard were silvery white but he looked lots younger than his eighty years. He was wearing a dark blue beret, apple green smock and sandals. His tanned face was lined with laugh wrinkles and his eyes were bright and lively.

"Too bad it's so foggy," he said. "On a clear day I can see one hundred fifty-six mountain peaks, and I've climbed all of them. This is the best view in the country! What brings you to Norway? Want to go treasure hunting?"

I explained briefly about Fred Coe's emerald and Uncle George was instantly alert. "You know," he said, "emeralds are so hard that only a few things will scratch them. That's the test—if it don't scratch, well then, you've got something."

Uncle George opened a drawer and took out a sharply pointed piece of quartz. "Are you sure it's all right for me to try this?"

I nodded, and held my breath as I heard an unmistakable sound: squeak . . . scratch! Howe looked up, his friendly face a perfect mask.

"Blackie, you have here a perfect emerald—colored—piece of g-l-a-s-s! That's all it is, just glass, but it's as clear and brilliant as the regal amethyst I found and sold to Tiffany. Did you ever hear about that?"

We hadn't; so Uncle George leaned back, deftly rolled a cigarette, and told for the thousandth time the story of his most valuable discovery.

It had been a warm Steptember day, before 1900. He had been roaming around the stone quarries on Pleasant Mountain, in Denmark, Maine, and one of the quarry men shouted, "Take a look in that crevice, Mr. Howe. I saw some good-looking quartz there yesterday."

So George crawled through the opening and entered a cave, and as soon as his eyes became accustomed to the darkness, he spied, high up on one wall, an outcropping of rock with quartz prisms. He climbed up, gave a few taps with his hammer, and down came the whole mass. He scooped up the pieces, put them in his basket and went home to examine them.

He had three fairly large stones and a few small ones. Where the first piece had broken off from the ledge, it was yellowish brown and kind of chalky, but turning it over he was delighted to find three large perfect prisms rising like pyramids, their color shading from pale pink to deep rose and he recognized his find as a rare type of purple amethyst.

He sent that specimen to the Agassiz Museum at Harvard University, and when I told this story on television in 1953, Professor Cornelius S. Hurlburt of the Department of Mineralogy lent me the stone to hold in front of the cameras.

Another piece, about the size of a plum, he cut down and polished to go in a brooch for his mother's fiftieth wedding anniversary. He made a frame from the gold nuggets he'd found at Swift River, and added twelve perfectly matched pearls from fresh-water clams.

The largest amethyst, when cleaned of its rough exterior, was a flawless stone of rich purple. It was so large and so beautiful that Uncle George mailed it to Tiffany in New York, with a letter asking if they would like to buy it, and if so, what they would pay.

Tiffany telegraphed back: "Will give you eight hundred fifty dollars for royal purple amethyst received today." Of course he accepted, and he was not surprised to learn later that Tiffany had sold the stone to J. Pierpont Morgan, who was collecting unusual gems.

In 1912 or 1913, as nearly as Uncle George could remember, the Morgan collection was shipped to Europe and put on display at a big international exhibition in Potsdam, Germany.

At this part of the story, Howe paused and gazed out of his big picture window toward the foggy landscape. We could barely see the lake below us and an occasional lofty pine loomed up like those in Japanese prints. The mountains were still obscured.

"A strange thing happened," he said, flicking his cigarette stub into the yawning fireplace and rolling another. "Thousands of people saw that stone, and someone must have mentioned it to the emperor. On the last afternoon of the exposition, a small party of German government officials was admitted. Heading the group was Emperor William the Second, better known to Americans as the Kaiser. He marched right up to the Morgan collection. His pointed mustache quivered and his hands trembled as he picked up my amethyst.

"He called the exhibition attendant and said excitedly, 'I must own this stone!'

"And as the clerk hesitated, he blurted out, 'Tell the owner I'll give ten thousand dollars for it!'"

Morgan was glad to sell. Thus did the purple amethyst

which George Howe had found in a Maine quarry become the property of the Kaiser.

"But why," I asked Uncle George, "did he offer so much for it?" That was the mystery, and the more I tried to figure it out, the more puzzled I became.

Returning to Boston, I immediately wrote Tiffany's. They recalled the transaction, but could add nothing to what I already knew. I went to the public library and brought home an armful of books on Germany, the Kaiser, and gems.

I had known that the Germans were fond of gems and regarded certain stones as having lucky powers, but I didn't know that their emperor—Friedrich Wilhelm Viktor Albert Hohenzollern—had his own personal collection which he cherished above everything else.

The Kaiser had bought the Maine amethyst only a few months before he flung his gray-green legions into Belgium in the opening days of World War I in 1914. On November 10, 1918, when it was clear that Germany had lost the war and that the Hohenzollern dynasty was ended, Kaiser Wilhelm, carrying his most valuable jewels with him, fled across the border to Holland, where he lived in exile in Doorn until June 4, 1941. He had come unscathed through the war despite his many enemies.

From one book I learned that the word amethyst comes from two Greek words meaning "not" and "intoxicating." The ancient Romans believed they could imbibe as much as they wished from an amethyst cup without becoming intoxicated. The Egyptians sometimes used amethyst drinking cups for their banquets and sometimes they baked the stones because heat changes the color from purple to yellow.

And then I struck pay dirt! "The Germans," I read, "have for centuries regarded the amethyst as having special, mystical powers. It is supposed to promote second sight and increase the gift of making prophecies. The man who wears a royal amethyst is immune from contagion or infection during epidemics, and military men who wear a royal amethyst *will be permanently protected from injury and death on the battlefield.*"

THE FIRST JAPANESE

Sometimes a little item that appears commonplace or routine turns out later to have been the beginning of an amazing story. Take this entry in the log of the whaling ship *John Howland*, out of Fairhaven, Massachusetts:

"Sunday June 27, 1841. This day light wind from S.E. The Isle in sight at 1 P.M. Sent two boats to see if there was any turtle. Found five poor distressed people on the Isle. Took them off. Could not understand anything from them more than they were hungry. Made lat. of the Isle 30.31N."

The log book of the *Howland* contains no further mention of the rescued men, although this entry appears under date of November 22:

"This day certain men were landed at Honolulu."

On June 27, 1841, Captain William H. Whitfield, master of the whaling ship *John Howland*, lying becalmed off the coast of Japan, picked up his telescope and swept the blue

Pacific for the hundredth time; but he saw nothing of interest. There was no land in sight, not a single sail, no spouting whales. Nothing but sky and water. It had been that way for weeks.

The *Howland* had sailed from her home port of Fairhaven, Massachusetts, on October 30, 1839, a year and a half earlier, and whales had proved uncommonly few and far between. Lacking the welcome call from the masthead, "Thar she blows!" the crew was becoming restless. They were bored with splicing ropes and making scrimshaw, and tired of eating "salt horse" and ship's biscuit with only an occasional plate of plum duff to break the monotony. They all eagerly looked forward to the day when the *Howland* would make a landfall in the Sandwich Islands (Hawaii) and they could go ashore, get some fresh fruit and vegetables, and then start the long voyage home.

Again Captain Whitfield scanned the limitless Pacific, now as flat and calm as his living-room table back home in Fairhaven. This time, he saw a black speck lying on the blue ocean, far off the starboard bow. An hour later he made out a cluster of high, black rocks, surf breaking around their base. Above them a number of birds were circling, their white wings flashing in the sun like the remnants of a tattered flag.

Captain Whitfield called to his mate, "Take a couple of boats and row over to those rocks! You may find some turtles or birds' eggs. Anyway, it'll give the men a chance to stretch their arms and legs."

Two boats were lowered over the side and soon the sailors from the *John Howland* were scrambling up the face of the rocks. They didn't see any turtles but they did find four famished Japanese fishermen. One of them, a boy about fourteen, had been burned almost black by the blistering sun; he could just lift his hand and point to his mouth to show that he wanted food and water. Their clothes were in rags, for they had been crawling over the barren rocks, existing on eggs and raw birds, for almost six months!

The sailors tenderly carried them to the boats, and rowed them to the *Howland* where Captain Whitfield himself administered sips of tea and soup. The fishermen were so grateful that tears trickled down their burned and wrinkled faces.

The *John Howland* went on about her business of catching whales, and five months later put in at the Sandwich Islands where four of the Japanese were landed at Honolulu. But the boy begged to stay with Captain Whitfield. He had made the captain understand that back in his native Japan he was known as Manjiro Nakahama, but that was too much for the crew, who called him John Mung. Manjiro pleaded that he wanted to go to America. The captain gave in, made him cabin boy and spent many hours teaching him to read and speak English, and how to navigate a whaling ship.

He was an apt pupil and learned rapidly. By the time the *John Howland* reached her home port of Fairhaven, Massachusetts, on May 7, 1842, he had picked up considerable knowledge that no other Japanese had ever learned—and *he was the first Japanese ever to set foot in the United States!*

Captain Whitfield was justly proud of him. Being a widower at the time, he arranged for Manjiro to board at the home of Eben Aiken, brother of the *Howland's* third mate. Later, when he married for a second time and established a home on Sconticut Neck, Whitfield took the young Japanese into his home and treated him like a son. He provided the boy with new clothes, books, and writing materials, and as soon as there was an opening, Manjiro was enrolled in the private school kept by Lewis Bartlett, and in short order he became head of his class. He was so anxious to get an education, he never went out to play at recess time, but stayed inside studying.

Captain Whitfield was a religious man, and every Sunday when he was at home he went to church. After the boy arrived, he too was taken to services, to the embarrassment of some of the congregation. They had never seen a lad like him, with such dark skin, flashing teeth, and slanted eyes. They resented the appearance of this "heathen" in the Whitfield pew, and openly said so.

The captain replied, "If they are that narrow-minded, I want no truck with them." So he left his family church, and changed over to the Unitarian where the Japanese was warmly welcomed.

When the captain was away at sea, Manjiro went to church with the Delano family. Captain Warren Delano (grandfather of Franklin Delano Roosevelt), being very fond of the studious young oriental, helped him with his studies. By this time, Manjiro had discovered Bowditch's *Navigator* and welcomed any help in deciphering it that he could get.

One thing Captain Whitfield insisted upon was that Manjiro should learn a trade, preferably one connected with whaling. There was an opening for an apprentice in one of the cooper shops and the boy grabbed it. In 1847, he had become such a good workman that he was given a berth on the bark *Franklin*, bound round the world on a three-year whaling voyage. Manjiro had been six years in Fairhaven; he was now nineteen or twenty.

There were two reasons why he wanted to make the voyage. First, he wanted to perfect himself in navigation. He served so well that he was promoted to first mate and became the first Japanese ever to navigate a ship by instruments. Being quick to learn, he also picked up valuable information about foreign currencies and the fundamentals of world trade.

Second, although the law forbade any Japanese citizen who had left the country ever to return, under penalty of beheading, he hoped that somehow he would have a chance to get back to Japan to see his mother—he still kept the kimono jacket she had made for him before he was ship-wrecked.

However, while the *Franklin* was at Guam, Manjiro wrote a letter to the Whitfields, expressing his gratitude for all they had done, and explaining that he had not been able to enter his native land. All Japanese ports were closed to foreign ships; but some day Manjiro hoped, every port in Japan would be open to all the nations of the world.

The *Franklin* returned to her home port with a profitable cargo of whale oil, and Manjiro raced to the Whitfield home. "We had a good voyage," he told the captain. "I like the work; my share was $350, which I give to you. At California, we hear much about gold mines. Everybody go there. Everybody get rich. I ask your permission to go to California and make fortune." He smiled eagerly. "Then maybe I can go back to Japan."

Captain Whitfield told Manjiro to keep the money, and got him a berth on a lumber ship bound for San Francisco. He stayed in the gold fields four months, until he had saved $600 more; then he worked his way to Honolulu and hunted up his former shipmates. One had died. Another was too scared to return to Japan. But the remaining two wanted to go with him.

Manjiro interviewed many captains, but could find no one who dared approach the forbidden land of Japan. Finally, he persuaded Captain Whitmore of the *Sarah Boyd*, bound for Shanghai, to take them along, agreeing that the Japanese would be dropped within sailing distance of their native shore.

For $100 Manjiro bought a whaleboat which he stocked with food, and with other things he thought would amaze the Japanese officials: axes, knives, window glass, and guns. For his mother, he took buttons, coffee, soap, sugar, and a sewing machine. He also packed a box of books, mostly on mathematics and navigation, including his greatest treasure of all, a copy of Bowditch's *Navigator*.

After many stormy weeks at sea, the *Sarah Boyd* reached the Luchu Islands. The whaleboat *Adventure* was lowered over the side with her three occupants, who commenced rowing for the distant shore. It was late afternoon. A gale was sweeping across the sea and thick wet snow was falling. Captain Whitmore waved goodbye to Manjiro Nakahama, and no white man saw him again for many years.

Then, in 1860, the Whitfields received a batch of mail from Honolulu. There was a long letter from Manjiro, saying that he was well, expressing his gratitude for all the things the Whitfields had done for him, and hoping they would visit him in Japan when the country was open to visitors. He had wanted to write before but could not get his letter out of Japan.

With this letter was another from Reverend Samuel Damon of The Seamen's Bethel, and an article Damon had written for *The Friend* magazine, published in Honolulu. Thus Captain Whitfield learned for the first time what had happened to the Japanese boy he had rescued and educated in Fairhaven—the Japanese boy who returned home, as no one before him had ever done; the first Japanese to visit American shores.

After the whaleboat *Adventure* left the side of the *Sarah Boyd* that stormy January day in 1850, the three Japanese rowed for ten hours before reaching an island. They anchored in the lee until daylight. Going ashore in the early morning, they were surprised that they could not understand the natives, and the natives could not understand them; for they had temporarily forgotten all Japanese words! Making signs that they wanted water, they were led to a pond where they bathed and boiled coffee. They cooked some beef American style, a dish which the natives had never seen before. When they had eaten, they were taken to the government office. The officials doubted they were Japanese; so chopsticks were brought. When Manjiro and his companions eagerly and deftly ate rice with them, they passed the test, and were officially declared to be Japanese. The arrival of these strangers was reported to the king of the Luchu Islands, who wanted to see them for himself.

He received them graciously enough but kept them prisoners for six months. They were then taken on a Japanese junk to the Island of Kyushu and turned over to another potentate. Every day Manjiro was questioned about the unknown country called America. He explained that where he'd been, boats were operated by steam, and he demonstrated the power of steam with a teakettle. He displayed the clock, compass and sewing machine he had brought. The revolutionary objects amazed and excited the Japanese.

After being interrogated over and over for forty-eight days, Manjiro's friends were allowed to go free, and returned to their families and obscure lives. Manjiro also wanted to visit his home, of course, but he was taken to Nagasaki and held for another thirty months answering questions. A thousand times he told his story of being rescued by Captain Whitfield. He directed the building of American-style boats, so different from Japanese junks, and showed how they could be navigated by scientific instruments.

He had been in Japan almost three years when he was allowed to visit his mother. Not having heard from her son for thirteen years, she believed him dead and had built a tomb to his memory. He stayed with her three days, and was then taken into custody again, and transported to Tokyo, where he was brought before the emperor himself. Once again he had to tell his story and demonstrate all the strange things he had brought from America. Kept under watchful guard, he feared that any day he might be beheaded; but he had such valuable information in his head that, instead, he found favor at the Imperial Palace.

From this time on, he rose rapidly until he was one of the most important men in Japan! First, he was given a post at the university in Tokyo, where he taught navigation; and a dozen scholars were assigned to help as he began the translation of Bowditch's *Navigator* into Japanese—a job that took seven years.

When Commodore Matthew C. Perry went from the United States to Japan in 1853 to negotiate a treaty which would open Japanese ports to all the nations of the world, Manjiro Nakahama acted as interpreter. No more suitable person could have been found in all Japan—he alone knew the American people and what they wanted to do. The documents were brought to him for translation and correction before they became official, and any blunder on Manjiro's part might have resulted in an international disaster. As it was, the Perry mission succeeded in opening Japan to worldwide commerce.

When the Franco-Prussian War broke out in 1870, Manjiro, an officer in the Imperial Navy, was sent to Europe to observe military operations and make suggestions that would improve the efficiency of the Japanese military and naval departments. While on this mission, his party was entertained at Washington, D. C., and he made a special trip to Fairhaven to call on Captain Whitfield. "Manjiro" was then forty-five years old, married, and had three of his seven children.

The eldest became a famous physician, Dr. Toichiro Nakahama, and after Captain Whitfield and Manjiro died, whenever Dr. Nakahama learned that friends or businessmen were coming to America, even if only to the Pacific Coast, he would say, "It is my wish that you go to Massachusetts and lay a wreath on the grave of my father's friend in Fairhaven."

He sent gifts galore, and it was he who requested Viscount Kikujiro Ishii to bring a samurai sword to Fairhaven. Just before Viscount Ishii left Tokyo to be ambassador at Washington, Dr. Nakahama called on him.

"Your Excellency," he said, "you know the story of my father's adventures. During his honorable life, gratitude and friendship for his benefactor never left his heart, as it shall never leave my heart, nor that of my children. It has long been my desire to present to the town of Fairhaven, Massachusetts, some object of art in appreciation of the kindness extended to my father Manjiro Nakahama. Do you think this can be arranged?"

Viscount Ishii agreed that it could. He interviewed President Woodrow Wilson and Honorable Charles S. Hamlin of the Federal Reserve Bank, and a great celebration was arranged for July 4, 1918.

New Bedford and Fairhaven were decorated with the Stars and Stripes, and, as far as I know for the first and only time in New England, public buildings also displayed the flag of the Rising Sun. American flags and Japanese flags were hung along the bridge between the two communities and flown from many private flagpoles.

At the outdoor exercises, Calvin Coolidge, lieutenant-governor of the commonwealth of Massachusetts, welcomed the Japanese dignitaries. Viscount Ishii presented the sword to Thomas W. Whitfield, grandson of Captain William Whitfield. And you can see it today in the Art and Music Room of Millicent Library, Fairhaven, along with a portrait of Manjiro Nakahama.

Every year until World War II, the Nakahamas in Japan and the Whitfields in Fairhaven—the children and the grandchildren—kept in touch with each other. They sent letters back and forth and always exchanged gifts at Christmas time. These two families, separated by everything that can separate human beings—space, language, religion, customs—were bound together for more than three generations by friendliness and understanding.

But as far as I can find out there is no member of the Whitfield family living in Fairhaven today, and since an atomic bomb was dropped on Nagasaki we have had no direct news from the Nakahamas.

THE MAN WITH A HOLE
IN HIS HEAD

W<small>HEN</small> twenty-five-year-old
Phineas P. Gage of Lebanon, New Hampshire, emerged
from the fortuneteller's on that sleepy September afternoon
in 1848, he didn't know whether to laugh, cry or just be
scared, for the silver coin which had crossed the grimy
palm of the gypsy woman had purchased a prophecy for
Phineas as provocative as it was perplexing.

It was encouraging to the country-bred young man to
learn that the future would find him traveling to far-off
places and making money, but he couldn't help being
disturbed when the gypsy said with a shudder, "You are
in immediate danger! Before the sun sets tomorrow, *the
icy fingers of death will touch you.* But you will survive.
You will go on the stage, and a hundred years from now,
people will still be talking about you."

"Nothing but balderdash!" Phineas told himself as he
rode through the autumn-tinted hills toward Cavendish,

Vermont, where as foreman of a construction gang he was working on the new main line of the Rutland & Burlington Railroad. Nevertheless, he did worry a little bit about the coming day, Saturday, September 13. "Lucky it isn't Friday the 13th!" he thought.

Saturday dawned fair and warm, and in midafternoon Phineas told his crew, "Gather up your tools, boys, and get ready to knock off. Soon's the last hole in that ledge has been drilled and loaded, we'll 'shoot her' and call it a day." Gage was an expert at blasting, always tamping the sand on top of the powder himself with a crowbar especially made for him by the company blacksmith.

When the deep-drilled holes had been filled with blasting powder and, Gage mistakenly supposed, topped off with sand, he straddled, crowbar in hand, and started tamping.

As he turned his head momentarily to give an order, the crowbar grazed the ledge, causing a spark which ignited the powder and set it off. A terrific explosion ensued, and through a cloud of flame, smoke and dust the tamping iron shot high into the air to land in a thicket some distance away. It was picked up by one of the crew who gasped, "Look at all the blood! And what's that stuff—brains?"

Gage lay flat on his back, badly burned but still conscious. Slowly he got to his feet, brushed the sparks from his smoldering clothes and with a blackened hand patted the top of his head where death had touched him. It felt wet and sticky and cold, but the jagged wound in his cheek was hot and painful and as he applied his blue bandanna to stop the flow of blood, it dawned on Phineas

P. Gage that his tamping iron had been blown by the explosion clear through his skull!

Fellow workers led Phineas to an ox cart, and unassisted he climbed in and leaned back against the seat for support. It was nearly a mile to the village of Cavendish, and as they plodded along over the rough country road, he must have recalled the gypsy's warning: "Danger! . . . but you will survive!" He spoke to the worried driver with forced cheerfulness: "I'll be all right soon's I get cleaned up and have a good night's rest."

They reached the hotel where Phineas boarded; he climbed out of the cart, walked unsteadily up the steps, sank into a rocking chair and said with understatement, "My head hurts!" Then, with only elbow assistance from a bystander, he climbed a long flight of stairs, unlocked the door to his room and lay down upon his bed.

Half an hour later Dr. J. M. Harlow arrived. He found Phineas suffering from second degree burns of hands and arms, and his face blackened with powder burns and dried blood, but it wasn't until the injured man had been cleaned up and had his scalp shaved that the doctor realized the seriousness of his situation. Phineas kept explaining, "My crowbar went right through my head," but Dr. Harlow only nodded sympathetically, charging the story to shock and delirium. However, as he washed away the coagula and shattered slivers of skull bone, he found a jagged hole approximating two and one-half by three inches, and was finally convinced the crowbar had entered Phineas' face just below the left eye, and passing obliquely upward, had crashed through his skull, taking a sizable portion of gray matter with it.

To make sure no other slivers of bone remained, Dr. Harlow inserted his left forefinger in the cheek wound, then passed his right index finger down through the hole in the top of the head, till his fingers touched, causing the patient no pain whatsoever. Gage grinned and said, "See! I told you so! And that tamping iron is a good-sized hunk of metal!"

And to be perfectly truthful, it was. The nonplused physician sent for the bar and noted its dimensions in his record: length, three feet seven inches; circumference at widest part, one and one-fourth inches; weight, thirteen and one-half pounds!

Convinced that no human could long live after a foreign body of that size had penetrated the brain, Dr. Harlow applied a simple dressing, ordered cold compresses, and left the victim propped up with pillows. A messenger was dispatched to Lebanon, New Hampshire, to notify Phineas' relatives to fetch his best suit, and the Cavendish undertaker was ordered to get a box ready.

Considering what he had gone through, Phineas had a fairly good night. Except for a blurry condition of the left eye and weakness from loss of blood, he was in excellent spirits, asking that his boss be assured he would be soon back on the job and requesting that his tamping iron be kept in a safe place.

The third day he showed signs of fever, so he was dosed with calomel and rhubarb, and when they had worked he felt much better. The fever went down and he slept comfortably, resting on his right side. At the end of a week he appeared to be gaining. He had a good appetite and asked for his folks and his fellow workmen. However, the sight in his left eye dimmed and in a few days was gone forever.

On October 11, Dr. Harlow asked Phineas, "Can you recall when you were hurt?"

And without hesitation, he replied, "Four weeks this afternoon at half past four o'clock, and if it's all right with you, Doc, I'd like to get up and take a little walk."

He tried the next day but was dizzy and went back to bed. On October 20, Gage got up, partially dressed himself and sat in a chair; three days later he put on all his clothes, went downstairs and out onto the street where he did some errands.

Dr. Harlow advised him strongly against exertion but a few days later, Phineas Gage bundled himself up, and with hot bricks from the hotel kitchen oven and blankets from the stable, he climbed in a covered carriage and was driven thirty miles through the snow-covered hills to his home in Lebanon.

He also took along his tamping iron and he spent endless hours telling his friends and relatives how it had been "blown clean through" his head. Grinning, Gage would say, "Didn't have too many brains before; only got half of 'em now!"

It was early April when he showed up at the railroad ready to go to work, but when advised his job as foreman had been filled, he sulked and said haughtily, "Then I'm going on the stage!" And off he stalked, crowbar on shoulder, for the bright lights of New York and Boston.

In a small tent on Boston Common, Phineas exhibited his head and the bar which had passed through it. Then he joined Austin & Stone's Museum, moving from that show to New York where the ubiquitous P. T. Barnum didn't let the fact that Phineas' skull was healed stop him from advertising: THE ONLY LIVING MAN WITH A HOLE IN HIS HEAD. The posters and one-sheets depicted a husky young man smiling broadly in spite of a huge iron bar which stuck out of his head. Actually, of course, the iron bar no longer protruded from Gage's head but he had it with him, and another skull, also perforated. During his side-show performances, he would shove the long iron through the holes in his extra skull to demonstrate just how he was injured. All the details were to be found in a pamphlet he sold, and by paying ten cents extra, skeptics could part Gage's hair and see his brain, what there was left of it, pulsating beneath the new, thin covering.

Believing that Phineas' recovery was the most remarkable on record, Boston's distinguished Dr. Henry F. Bigelow, professor of surgery at Harvard University, prepared an article for the July, 1850, issue of the *American Journal of Medical Sciences,* only to find himself scoffed at and ridiculed for being so gullible.

"You don't really believe a three-foot iron crowbar went through that man's brain, now do you?"

But Dr. Bigelow did believe it and in 1851 he brought Phineas to Boston and put him up at his own expense so that doubting members of the medical profession could see for themselves a man whose head had been punctured and who had survived to laugh about it. Doctors, interns, nurses and the press came day after day to see for themselves.

With all of this publicity, Phineas Gage made good money, but he was restless, and after roaming from circus to side show and back again, he settled in Hanover, New Hampshire, working as horse handler for Jonathan Currier. While there he met a man buying horses for a stage line in Chile, South America. Phineas joined him and went along to look after the animals, and after a year among the mountains back of Valparaiso, he graduated to stage driver, skillfully handling six or more spirited steeds as they hauled a lurching coach up and down the tortuous mountain roads.

In 1859 Phineas' health took a sudden turn for the worse. He quit the stage coaches and mountain passes and sailed on a clipper ship bound for California, where his aged mother was living in San Francisco. He suffered terribly from seasickness and arrived in broken health so that he was able to do only light work thereafter. On May 21, 1861, he died suddenly—twelve years, six months, and eight days after the thirteen and one-half pound iron bar had blasted through his brain in Cavendish, Vermont.

When news of his death reached Boston, all of the medical men who knew of Gage's accident and his remarkable recovery bemoaned the fact that no autopsy had been made, and because this case was so unusual a request was forwarded to the family, asking that Phineas' skull be preserved in the interest of medical science.

With the help of the mayor of San Francisco, this was accomplished. The body was exhumed, the skull removed and sent back east to Harvard College where it has remained in the medical museum ever since, along with the tamping iron which punctured Gage's brain. I have seen these grisly objects many times and am frank to confess that it still seems impossible an object of that length and weight could pass through a man's head without killing him.

While the gypsy fortune teller did prophesy that Phineas would "go on the stage and travel to far places," after his brush with death, she omitted to say that because of the accident he would gradually change from a simple country man to a loudmouthed, boisterous and very profane individual—so profane the police drove him from Boston Common and even strong men of those rugged times quaked when they heard him.

He developed an attachment for the tamping iron which nearly split his skull. He kept it well polished and always close by his side. And no wonder—what all men seek, Phineas Gage had attained by means of his crowbar. In his way he was absolutely unique!

LANGDON MOORE

Whenever I get weary of these modern, complicated who-dun-its with their impossible characters and abstruse plots, I take from the bottom shelf of my bookcase a battered volume of police records published way back in 1866. It is entitled *Professional Criminals of America* and was written by Thomas S. Byrnes, chief detective of the New York City police department.

Because of its four hundred pages, this is a heavy, hard-to-handle book, but I never fail to get a kick out of the minute descriptions of old-time crooks and female scalawags, and the clever methods they used in their business. The two hundred illustrations are not the usual half-tone cuts or line drawings, but actual heliotypes, exactly like the prints which then made up the Rogues' Gallery. Some of the subjects resemble the lowdown characters they were, but mostly they look just like my favorite aunts and uncles in our gold-edged family album.

One of the more intelligent-appearing, well-dressed thugs

is Langdon W. Moore, who was born in 1830 to a family of farming folks up in East Washington, New Hampshire. In a year, the family moved to Newburyport, Massachusetts, and there in the seaport town, Langdon spent most of his boyhood. When he was ten and attending the Kent Street Grammar School, he was mistakenly accused of some petty misdemeanor by the school master, "Bully" Titcomb, who attempted to strike him with a ruler. Langdon dived between the master's legs, leaped to the top of a desk, made a successful handspring through an open window and landed unhurt on the ground below. He was never inside a school room again.

Langdon said, "I'm almost eleven and ready for work," so his father sent him to a near-by farm where an elderly man and his sister bargained to bring him up. They promised to give him his board and room and suitable work clothes in return for the chores he would do. "You can study," the old lady said, "in your spare time."

But the boy soon found that getting up winter mornings around four o'clock and milking cows by candle light, then sawing, splitting and stacking wood and doing all the other chores, left no time for his studies, and he never did have a moment for relaxation and fun. So he ran away.

Shortly after this he was apprenticed to David Ash of Lisbon, New Hampshire. "If ye'll stay till you're twenty-one, I'll give you a 'freedom suit,' one hundred dollars and a couple of my best heifers." Langdon agreed, but the drudgery of farm life and lonesomeness were more than he could stand. Again he quit and by bumming his way through the snow-covered country he arrived at East Boston where his father was living with his second wife and the other children. Langdon was now seventeen—a tall, sturdy, independent young man with very definite ideas.

He liked the hustle and bustle of the city and soon got a job in a boot and shoe store, but that proved too confining. He then bought up a small grocery which failed, and after paying every dollar he owed to his creditors he set out for New York. Because he didn't want his folks in New England to know where he was and what he was doing, Langdon Moore assumed the alias of Charles A. Adams, and he is listed under that name in Inspector Byrnes' book, *Professional Criminals of America*.

The gang he went around with were mostly rowdies who introduced the country lad to smoking, drinking and gambling. He told a friend, "This is the life for me." And he added, "But there is no honor among thieves. All these gamblers cheat each other."

As time went on, Moore himself became proficient at various "games." He was especially lucky at faro and played heavily. One Saturday night at a gambling joint on West Broadway, he had his first stroke of luck. He had gone there with his landlord, a Yankee from New Bedford, who, losing his money, borrowed from Moore. Langdon had been winning at every play and continued to win all night. When they returned to the boarding house on Sunday morning, the man said to his wife, "Mary, yesterday this boy was just our boarder; now Charley owns this house and all the furniture. I've been playing faro and lost. He played and won."

"Well," shrugged the woman, "you have to lose once in a while."

Flushed with this touch of beginner's luck, Moore played again and again, and soon had more money than any of the poor New Hampshire farmers for whom he had worked. He became manager, then owner, of a small saloon and gambling house at 23 Mercer Street, New York. He added poker to his accomplishments, cheated when he had to, and was cheated in turn by some of the most notorious underworld characters. From these flashy new acquaintances he heard about an even easier way to make money.

Counterfeiting was an exciting game for Moore and it fascinated him. He began by peddling the "queer" made by others. Then, having been bitten by the bug, he tried making big bills out of little ones, and as his handicraft was better than most, he succeeded admirably. Still posing as Charley Adams, Moore worked alone, cutting, pasting and printing the defunct bills he purchased from banks that had failed.

On the morning of February 19, 1856, Moore and a man named Marsh left New York for Boston. With them they carried a whole suitcase stuffed with phony ten dollar bills. They had agreed not to start "pushing the queer" until two days later but Marsh was so anxious to see how much stuff he could palm off on the dumb Bostonians, he unloaded two hundred dollars in various saloons and cafés the first night.

The counterfeit money was quickly detected and the police notified. They traced Marsh to his hotel room and both men were dragged from their beds, arrested on suspicion and carted to the station house. Marsh was identified and convicted; Moore, after three months in Charles Street jail, was acquitted.

Infuriated by Marsh's carelessness, Moore could scarcely contain himself. When his father visited him in jail and said, "Now I hope you'll get into some kind of respectable work," Langdon declared angrily, "I'll never do another day's work unless I am compelled to do it for the state!" And he never did.

Instead, he plunged even deeper into counterfeiting. He secured the latest type of copying press, several cases of fancy type and a great quantity of special inks. He learned how to dissolve the printed name of one bank and cleverly substitute another, and after considerable practice he could forge other men's signatures so expertly they themselves could not tell the difference.

To prove this, Langdon Moore boldly marched into the Shoe & Leather Bank in New York City and handed the cashier one of his handmade one hundred dollar bills, saying, "I wish you would examine this and tell me if it is genuine." The cashier placed the counterfeit bill before the president, who looked closely, smelled and felt of it and then gravely announced, "Of course this is genuine. I'd know my own signature anywhere."

Quite often, the men who worked for Moore as "push-ers" brought in stolen bonds, jewelry and other valuables, but he would never handle any watches or diamond stick pins and so forth until he knew the man who had lifted them and from whom they had been stolen. Under no circumstances would he ever accept goods which had been taken at the point of a gun or by other force.

His counterfeit money was in great demand; business increased and he made a fortune. Then, hearing by the grapevine that Secret Service men were on his trail, he looked about for a suitable hideout. In 1857 he bought a farm in Natick, Massachusetts, not far from the present Worcester Turnpike. Here he posed as a well-to-do New York sportsman, keeping hunting dogs and a pair of fast trotting horses. His guns were made to order by McFarland of New York and he used only the very best of fishing equipment. Each spring and fall, Moore would invite some of his friends and business associates to spend a few weeks at the farm, and with them he would hunt, fish and keep out of sight. The country neighbors thought him a bit stand-offish, but ascribed that to his being such a big businessman in such a big city as New York.

Finally there came a day when he had enough of the counterfeit game. He sold out his New York gambling joint, discharged his gang of "shovers" and began the study of bank robbing, which eventually led to fame, fortune and prison. Of course he wanted to study the very latest in bank locks, so he purchased several of the new Yale locks from Herring & Co. of New York, but he was un-

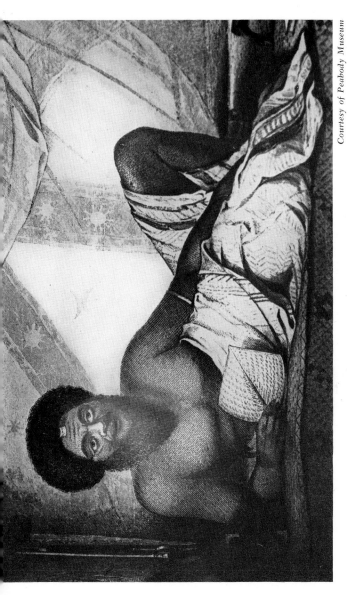

Thakombau, King of all the Fiji Islands. Credited with having eaten many of his enemies, he later renounced cannibalism and joined the church. His wig, palm leaf fan and a tooth are exhibited at the Peabody Museum, Salem. (*Captains and Cannibals*)

An old woodcut showing the first elephants being loaded aboard a sailing ship for transportation to Salem, Massachusetts. *(Captains and Cannibals)*

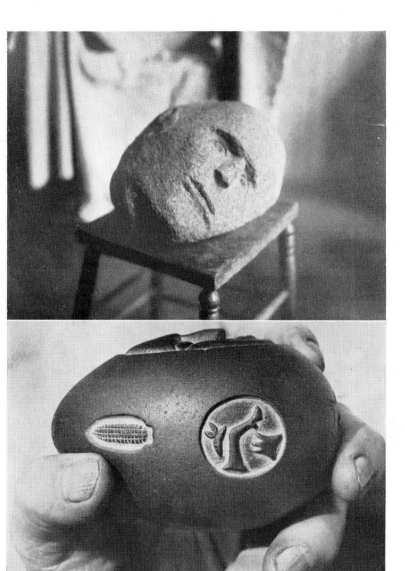

(Upper) The Essex Stone Head as it looks today in the Peabody
Museum, Salem, Mass. *(Unexpected Finds)*

(Lower) The New Hampshire Indian Mystery Stone with designs
pertaining to American Indians. *(Unexpected Finds)*

(*Left*) Manjiro Nakahama, the first Japanese to come to America. (*The First Japanese*)
(*Right*) Captain William H. Whitfield of Fairhaven, Mass., who brought the first Japanese to this country. (*The First Japanese*)

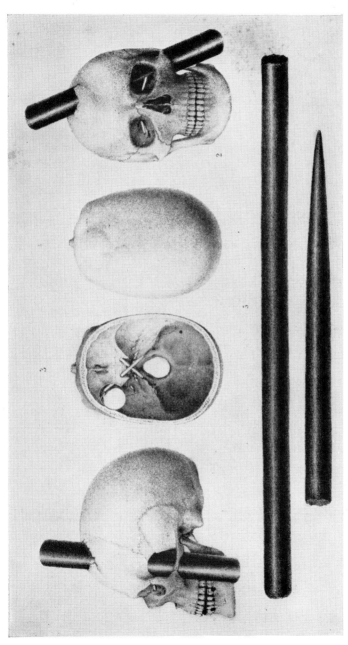

Drawings from the medical report on Phineas Gage, showing how an iron bar passed through his skull without killing him. (*The Man with a Hole in His Head*)

A portrait of Langdon Moore as he looked when he carried out his famous bank robberies. *(Langdon Moore)*

Remains of the farmhouse in Rindge, New Hampshire, showing the secret tunnel the artist Smith may have used to escape after painting his murals. (*Two Wanderers*)

One of the few existing photographs of the Wild Men of Borneo, Wano, *left*, and Plutano, *right*, with their manager Mr. Hannaford Warner. *(Side Shows)*

A. H. Blackington

The Old Stone Mill with the curved rails marking the site of the original 500 feet of Joe Cushing's railroad. (*Joe Cushing*)

Aunt Emmeline Benner Lewis, in whose house a pirate treasure map was found, shown on her one hundredth birthday. (*The Pirate's Treasure*)

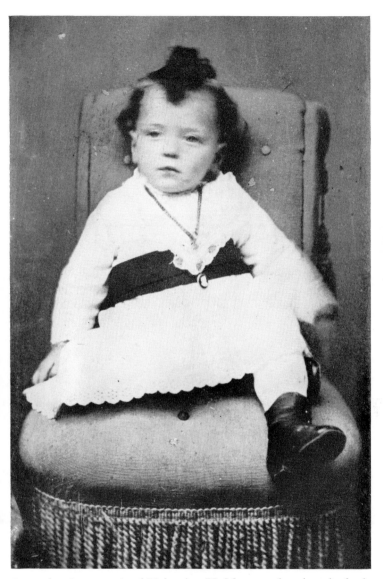

An early photograph of Valentine H. Marston showing the lock of hair on his forehead by which his ghost was identified. (*First-Hand Ghosts*)

Davis

The *Kronprinzessin Cecilie* photographed shortly after she slipped into Bar Harbor, Maine, with a cargo of nearly $15,000,000 of bullion at the declaration of World War I. (*The Kronprinzessin Cecilie*)

The *Kronprinzessin Cecilie*, converted into the troopship *Mount Vernon*, as she returned to Boston Harbor, Mass., with the victorious 26th (Yankee) Division at the end of World War I. *(The Kronprinzessin Cecilie)*

Howard Nichols' great barn and residence shortly after completion in 1922, showing the cars of sight-seers. (*Howard Nichols' Barn*)

Howard Nichols and his daughter, Christine, photographed in 1941. (*Howard Nichols' Barn*)

A. H. Blackington

The waterfall at Rocky Gorge where Dottie Sparkes was trapped for five hours.

(*Miracle of Rocky Gorge*)

able to buy a new Lillie lock so he went to that company's salesroom on Broadway, forced the door and helped himself.

He practiced taking these locks apart and putting them back together until he could do it with his eyes closed, and he knew what was going on inside them just by the sound. Now he wanted some big safes to work on; he purchased three which he had shipped to Natick. There in his well-equipped work room, he learned how to open them by half a dozen methods. Then, not caring to have them around the farm, he filled up the holes he had bored, gave them fresh coats of paint and sent them away to be sold at auction.

On his next trip to New York, where he still posed as Charles Adams, Langdon met up with a couple of old pals, "Dutch" Dan and Ned Livingston. They confided they were going to rob the savings bank in Francestown, New Hampshire, and offered to cut him in if he would act as outside man—that is, stand guard to give the signal if anyone approached.

Without thinking, Moore agreed to help, but later his conscience bothered him about robbing poor people of their savings. He wanted to back out but he had given his word and he needed both ready cash and experience in his new field of bank robbing. So he met the New York crooks and drove them to Francestown to look things over. He was even more against the job when he noted that Dutch Dan and Livingston were passing a bottle of whisky. He hated liquor and none of his other pals ever took a sip when they were on the job. The three men "piped" the bank and decided it would be a cinch. Ned and Dan returned to New York; Moore took a train to Boston.

Unknown to his friends, he hunted up an old pal, Harry Howard, better known to the police as "English" Harry. He said, "Look, I want you to help me. All you've got to do is put on a cop's uniform and walk up and down in front of the bank in Francestown, New Hampshire. If you'll do this next Saturday night, I'll give you one hundred dollars."

The following Saturday, Dan and Livingston arrived in Nashua as agreed, and Moore was waiting to drive them to Francestown. They arrived after dark and tethered the horse under some trees. Only a few lights twinkled in the houses along the square, then were extinguished as the country folks went to bed.

About eleven o'clock, just as the boys were getting ready to break into the bank, Howard showed up wearing a policeman's long coat and carrying a lantern which he flashed into all the store windows as he tried their doors. The New Yorkers were surprised and disappointed. Moore said, "We'll wait until he goes away," but he did not go; he sat down on some near-by steps and played with a mongrel puppy.

The hours dragged on, and at last Moore said, "Well, the night is most gone. We'll have to try this some other time. You drive the wagon to the foot of the hill and wait for me. I want to see just what time this flatfoot does quit."

Disgruntled and grumbling and passing their bottle more often, the two robbers drove out of the village. Moore crossed the square and whispered to Howard. "Good work! Here's your money." Then he joined the others, who never suspected the cop was a fake.

Langdon Moore saw his pals aboard the milk train that Sunday morning and smiled with satisfaction when he noted Howard, now minus his policeman's uniform, peacefully snoozing in the rear seat of the smoking car.

Moore's next job, actually his first bank robbery, was probably the cleverest and slickest ever committed in this country. For persistent planning and perfect timing it had no equal until the 1950 robbery of Brinks Inc. in Boston's North End. This modern haul was described by radio commentators and reporters as "fantastic" and was compared to the stunt Langdon Moore pulled when he robbed the National Bank of Concord, Massachusetts, practically singlehanded in 1865. I gave to the United Press a brief account of that old robbery, which was printed in newspapers all over the United States. But of course there was a great deal more to it than that.

The Francestown fiasco occurred on a Saturday night, and it was noon of the following Monday when Moore stopped in Concord, Massachusetts, to get a bite to eat.

While there, he saw the cashier of the Concord National Bank return from his lunch, unlock the front door and ascend the stairs, leaving the key in the lock. Moore crossed the street and went upstairs to the bank. He laid a genuine hundred dollar bill on the counter and politely asked for some change. He closely watched the cashier open first the vault and then the inner burglar box. From this quick appraisal he figured that the bank could be entered and cleaned out completely by anyone who was smart and who kept his wits.

Moore knew that he would need some help and immediately thought of Harry Howard who had done such a fine job playing policeman. So he invited Howard to come to the farm for a "vacation" and together they drove to Concord to "case" the Concord bank. While Langdon was upstairs getting change and looking around, Howard stayed in the front entry pressing a gob of wax around the door key. Then they drove to Boston and bought a bunch of blank keys, one of which, in Langdon's Natick work shop, they carefully filed to fit the wax impression.

Returning to Concord the next night they tried their new key. It fitted the lock very nicely but would not throw back the bolt. Disappointed, they went home, made another key and returned to the bank to try that one. It still would not work, so Howard went out and found a long ladder which he placed against the rear wall, and climbed up. He forced open a window, descended the stairs, removed the bolts from the front door lock, took it off and admitted Moore. By the slit of light from their dark lantern, they inspected the lock. A small steel spring in the back protruded just enough to prevent an ordinary key from working, so Moore filed down the spring, put the lock back on the door and tightened the bolts. The pair then went out the window, down the ladder, and were

soon on their way to the Natick farm, well satisfied with
that night's work.

On their next trip to Concord, the robbers boldly entered
the front door and tramped upstairs. The door that led
to the main office gave them no trouble and they turned
toward the big vault. Here they found something they
had never anticipated; this huge, smooth, black steel vault
had five keyholes! They were stymied again!

Howard wanted to quit but Moore was determined to
keep at it. In a few days he drove to Boston and visited
every store where safes were sold or vaults were on display. Finally he found what he was looking for, a vault
practically the same as the one in the Concord bank. He
blandly explained that he was an insurance man and needed
a new vault for his office; the accommodating clerk showed
him how everything worked, carefully explaining that *the
locks were interlocked and no two keys were alike.* Moore
was profuse with his thanks and promised to call again.

Harry Howard was thoroughly disgusted. He pointed
out that they had already wasted several weeks fooling
with locks, keys and ladders, and added, "It takes us half
the night driving twenty-four miles back and forth between Concord and Natick."

Moore agreed and placidly suggested that they set up
a work bench somewhere handy.

"Just where could we set up shop and be handy—and
unnoticed?"

"Why," said Moore calmly lighting one of his expensive
cigars, "I see no reason for not working right in the bank.

There's a closet behind the vault where we could keep our tools, and that'll be very handy."

And can you believe it? That's exactly what they did. Practically every other night for the next six months, they let themselves in, marched upstairs and worked until three in the morning making and fitting keys to the big vault. As fast as one key was finished and found to work, Langdon would rub his hands and whisper, "Good! Now, my friend, we are making progress!"

When the last of the five keys was perfected and the big door swung open, another black wall of steel faced them, this one with two keyholes. However, it took only two weeks to make keys for that, and then they examined the heavy burglar box. Howard suggested they carry it to the window, dump it on the ground, and rob the bank that very night, but Moore exclaimed, "That's not sportsmanlike! Any fool can break in and clean out a vault under cover of darkness, when no one's looking. I want to rob this one in the daytime!"

And besides, he also wanted to make sure that it would be profitable.

About the first of September, Moore paid another visit to Concord, called at the bank and asked the cashier if he had any "seven-thirty" notes. He explained that he was administrator of a large estate and was selling land, converting the money into the "seven-thirties" because he figured they were a good investment.

The cashier nodded. "I have only a few today, but if

you will come in next week I expect to have sixty-five thousand dollars' worth."

While Moore was carrying on this conversation, he learned one very important thing: the cashier unlocked the vault with seven special keys which he carried in his pocket, but the key to the burglar box was kept on a tiny shelf inside the vault! Langdon went out feeling pretty proud, and he told Harry Howard, "We'll pull it off next week. Now I suggest we take a little vacation."

So that afternoon, Langdon opened up a bundle of "queer" he had made and gave Howard fifteen hundred dollars in phony bills "to have a good time with." He took five thousand. They agreed to meet at the Natick farm on the coming twenty-fourth of September, 1865.

On Monday the twenty-fifth, after shaving and dressing in their best clothes, the two men hitched the sorrel mare into a phaeton purchased especially for this one job and drove out of the yard headed toward Boston. But in a short while they turned left and took a back road which led over the hills to the Wayland turnpike, arriving in Concord just before noon.

Resplendent in his high shiny silk hat and fashionable long coat, Moore got out of the phaeton and entered the historic cemetery where he pretended to be examining the moss-grown headstones. He watched dignified George F. Heywood, president of the bank, drive up and hitch his horse. Heywood, with his picturesque burnside whiskers and plug hat, was as familiar a sight in Concord as was Emerson, Hawthorne or Thoreau, and just as important.

Moore meandered around among the gravestones until Heywood came out and walked up Main Street. When the cashier, John M. Cheney, left the bank to get his lunch, Harry Howard, who was waiting in the carriage, drove to a near-by grocery store where he bought a pound of ten-penny nails. Langdon walked quickly down the sidewalk and stepped into the front entrance of the bank, using his key to open the door. He was about to close it behind him when he heard a childish voice say, "Let me in! I want to see my daddy!" and there stood a little girl with pigtails, one scuffed shoe shoved into the doorway. Langdon patted her head kindly. "There's a directors' meeting going on upstairs now. Come back in half an hour." And he breathed a sigh of relief when she ran down the street, satisfied.

Quickly he bolted the door, dashed up the stairs two at a time, unlocked the door at the head of the stairs and entered the main office. The hands of the clock pointed to ten minutes past twelve.

With nimble fingers he fitted the five keys into the outside vault door, then two others into the inner door, and reaching up on the shelf found the key that fitted the burglar box. From under his coat he pulled a meal bag, shook it open and poured into it the entire contents of the burglar box, which he then relocked, and pocketed the key. Then he scooped up all the packages of money he could find—great handfuls tied in bundles—and dumped those in the bag. When he had completely cleaned the vault, he shut the doors and locked them, skipped across the sunlit office and down the stairs.

Stepping outside, he met several women and turned so that they could see only part of his face. Nonchalantly he lighted a cigar with steady hands, then, lifting the heavy bag to his shoulder, he walked slowly down the street and joined Howard in the carriage. They drove out of town at a most leisurely gait, but a half mile farther on Moore touched the mare with the whip and she struck up a four-minute clip with her head high and tail over the dasher, and they went through Wayland flying.

They arrived at the Natick farmhouse without attracting attention. Howard unharnessed the mare, and in just one hour from the time they left Concord, she was rolling in the dirt back of the house, removing all traces of the hot twelve-mile ride. Moore grabbed a bushel basket, placed the meal bag inside it and carried it unconcernedly to his chamber.

Then he undressed, jumped into bed and shouted for his sister, telling her that he was sick and needed a doctor— the nearest one was in Natick village, almost three miles away. No sooner had she departed than Langdon jumped up and quickly dumped the contents of the bag on his bed. It was a staggering sight! The first package he opened contained nearly ninety-one thousand dollars' worth of coupon bonds. Then came a roll of paper containing the greater part of the sixty-five thousand dollars' worth of "seventy-thirty" bonds, fresh from the United States treasury. All told, he had scooped up three hundred and

[95]

ten thousand dollars in cash, securities, and valuables, besides some trinkets and jewels.

This was divided equally, Howard wrapping his share into small bundles which he concealed under his clothes. Moore hid his part of the loot under hay in the stable and went back to bed.

When the doctor arrived, he found Mr. Moore perspiring freely, with a slight fever and apparently in great pain. He left some pills, ordered a light diet and complete rest. The patient was able to be up early the next day, however. He went to the haymow and removed the bundles of loot. Placing the money in several large Mason preserving jars which he stuffed into an old rubber boot, he crammed the rest into a four-gallon stone butter jar, and buried the whole boodle near the stump of a hemlock tree half a mile from the house and in plain view of the kitchen window.

For this bold daylight robbery, neither Moore nor Howard nor anyone else ever spent a single day in prison. When Mr. Heywood was told that his bank had been robbed at noon of over three hundred thousand dollars, his whiskers stood right out straight. He got in touch with the Boston police and Chief Kurtz sent Detectives Hunt, Heath and Jones to Concord to investigate. Moore was suspected and questioned and finally made a sharp deal. "Some officials of the Concord Bank were directed to me and after considerable haggling with their lawyers, I got them to sign an agreement never to prosecute either Howard or myself, and later I turned over to them exactly two hundred and three thousand dollars in negotiable securities."

It was but one of many such deals that Moore got away with during his career.

Because he worked with such neatness and skill, his jobs were recognized by the police but they never could pin anything on him. Inspector Thomas S. Byrnes wrote, "Moore was a mechanical genius. He learned that the makers of a well-known safe had perfected a burglar-proof safe, so he purchased two of them, took them apart and re-assembled them. Then, obtaining a list of every bank in New England which had installed these safes, he made a circuit of New England and robbed every one of them."

He was shadowed by detectives, called in for questioning and continually under suspicion. Altogether he robbed well over one hundred banks, stores, hotels and big business offices, but he was not apprehended until some associates bungled a job in Rockland, Maine, in 1870.

Alden Litchfield, a local merchant, and Addison Kaiser, the city marshal, conspired to rob the Lime Rock Bank, and through connections with crooks in New York they secured the services of Langdon Moore. As Rockland is at the end of a long peninsula, Moore demanded a boat be secured for their getaway, but none could be found. When he heard this, Moore had the same feeling of reluctance, or "hunch," he had felt about the Francestown, New Hampshire, job years before, but he agreed to engineer the robbery nevertheless. The crooks broke through the telegraph office next door and got into the bank. Being unable to crack the big safe by other means, they prepared to blow it open. But in their haste they spilled a quantity of powder on the floor, and when the fuse was touched off, the powder exploded prematurely, almost knocking the whole gang onto Rockland's Main Street.

Moore and another man were caught by a sheriff's posse as they drove toward Augusta. Some of the gang had made their way to Belfast but soon they were all rounded up and one confessed. The trial was exciting and speedy. Moore was convicted and sentenced to the Maine State Prison at Thomaston and he served, I believe, six years.

In the prison workshop, Langdon learned to make carriages, and as he always did, he gave the work the best he had. One day the warden sent for him. "Mr. Moore," he said, "your carriages sell for a higher price than any others because they're better made. From now on, I want you to sign them so we can prove to customers they're your handiwork."

Normally, Moore would have taken pride in this and been greatly amused by it. But he was too deeply resentful over a special grievance that he had. Always fastidious in his personal appearance, he was furious that he had to wear such disreputable clothing in prison. While clean as he could manage, his clothes were little better than a mass of rags and patches. His pleas for a new work suit went unheeded, and thereby hangs a tale still recounted by officers at Thomaston.

Every Sunday morning the prisoners were marched to the chapel for morning services, and a guard was stationed in the yard to turn back any man who appeared too ragged or unkempt to appear in public—for there were always prison officials, some womenfolk, politicians, and so forth visiting chapel. On one Sunday early in 1876, the guard spotted Moore clad in his rags and tatters and motioned him to drop out of line. Although it was strictly against the rules, Moore said firmly, "If these clothes are good enough for me to wear in the work house, they are good enough for me to wear in the house of the Lord." And he jumped forward into the chapel.

After the service, as the convicts were leaving, Moore signaled the man behind him to hold back a bit, leaving an open space. Turning so that his back was toward a group of prison officers and their wives, Moore dropped his cap on the ground. When he bent over to pick it up, the whole seat of his trousers pulled loose, exposing his under clothing in rags and a sizable section of his posterior. There were a few muffled chuckles and gasps, and all the prisoners figured it "would cost Moore his life."

Next day he was taken to the guardroom where three inspectors were waiting. They asked if he had any other clothes, and upon learning that he had, dispatched an attendant to fetch them. When the bundle was opened and found to contain shirts and drawers too ragged and worn to be of any use, one of the officials said, "That's all, Mr. Moore. We will speak to the warden. You may go."

That afternoon, Langdon was taken to the tailor shop and measured for a complete new suit, double-soled calfskin boots and a brand new cap. His fellow inmates declared they would willingly go to chapel naked if so doing would get them such a handsome outfit.

Finally he was set free. When he reached his home in New York his wife didn't know him, he had grown so old and lost so much weight. His six-year-old daughter, whom he had never seen, was scared of him. After a few days of catching up with things, Langdon sold all his furniture at auction and moved his family to Boston where he immediately engaged in a new series of crimes. Apparently he robbed bank after bank with the greatest of ease.

In 1880, the year he was fifty years old, he ran into real trouble. Charged with attempting to rob the Warren Institution for Savings in Charlestown, Massachusetts, he was sentenced to a long term in prison. Although he insisted he was innocent and had been framed by the police, he philosophically felt that since he had committed so many crimes and gone free, maybe this was his just punishment. He settled down behind the high walls of Concord Prison, only a short distance from where he pulled his first successful job.

When Concord Prison was turned into a reformatory in December, 1884, the inmates were transferred to Charlestown, described by Moore as "an ancient bastille, filthy and unfit for hogs." As always when he was in custody, Moore did his work, kept his mouth shut, and made no trouble unless he or someone else was treated unfairly. He became interested in prison reform and was able to bring about a number of improvements in the care of prisoners. Especially he insisted, "An honest man should keep his word given to a crook just as much as if he gave it to another honest man."

All this time, of course, he was growing older, and his health had been undermined by his many years behind the bars; but there was life in the old boy yet. When he was released on September 8, 1890, having served ten and a half years for a crime he claimed he did not commit, he went at once to headquarters to call upon the police officials and detectives whom he had kept busy during his eventful career as counterfeiter and bank robber.

With his usual impressive dignity, he said, "I have come to tell you personally that I am out of stir, so you won't have to pay any stoolpigeon fifty cents for this information. And don't worry about me any more; I've learned my lesson and from now on *I am going straight!*"

Which he did! He visited old friends whom he had not seen in years, paid up every back bill that he owed, and prepared a series of lectures which he gave before boys' clubs and civic groups, on the subject "Crime Does Not Pay."

Then he finished the book he'd been writing—a complete confession of his exciting life as America's Public Enemy Number One. This sturdy volume, of 659 pages with many illustrations, was privately printed and went on sale in 1893. It was especially popular with the country's police and government agents who hoped to get information about crooks they hadn't been able to catch and also knowledge of the way a criminal thinks and acts.

No one noticed when Langdon Moore disappeared. No one knew where he had gone, but the police didn't bother to hunt. He had given them his word of honor that he was quitting his old life, and furthermore no recent robbery had the touch of genius for which he was famous. He simply dropped out of sight.

When, in 1927, I tried to find out what had become of this spectacular Yankee, I ran against a blank wall. The files of Greater Boston newspapers had nothing about Moore after his release. I visited several old police chiefs and detectives but they could tell me nothing. I couldn't find when he died, or where he is buried.

I wanted to own a copy of his book, but these too had vanished except for a few in police libraries and probably family attics in Maine and New Hampshire.

Then one night in 1945 at the conclusion of a radio broadcast concerning the daring daylight robbery of the Concord bank, I asked if any listener knew what ever became of Langdon W. Moore. Within forty-eight hours I had a stack of letters—pieced together they gave me the missing story. I was dumfounded! Moore had returned to the scenes of his boyhood days in New Hampshire, and in the little village of West Swanzey, a few miles from his birthplace, he had been welcomed and befriended by the lovable old playwright Denman Thompson!

I have been to West Swanzey several times and I've talked to many who were acquainted with either Denman Thompson or Moore or both, and still there is no satisfactory explanation as to why Thompson did what he did for Moore. They could not have been boyhood friends, because Denman came to New Hampshire when he was fourteen in 1847—the year that Langdon Moore went to work in Boston. There is no record that they met around 1850 when Thompson appeared as an extra on the stage of Boston's famous Old Howard theater off Scollay Square, but they could have. They may have met in any number of places during the following years while Thompson was playing minor roles in the theater and Moore was traveling a good deal "on business." Perhaps it was later, in Canada. Thompson made his home in Toronto for several years, and in 1868 Langdon fled there and lived for a while at the Rassin House.

I had a long talk with an old neighbor of Denman Thompson's recently, and he believes they became acquainted in Canada. He also advanced the idea that Langdon Moore—flush with cash he had obtained by palming off his "queer" money or rich beyond his dreams with silver and gold stolen from some carelessly protected country bank—may have loaned Thompson a few thousand dollars to tide him over hard times. It is true there were many years when Thompson never had enough money. He had no luck at all until he began to write his own plays—and the first one he wrote was *the story of a young man accused of robbing a bank!*

Then he wrote the *Old Homestead*, which became a sudden national success. It is said that he starred in the role of "Josh Whitcomb" no less than fifteen thousand times! Thompson made a fortune from this play, and he became so famous that a letter with simply his name on it would be delivered to him. Although the *Old Homestead* was first presented in 1886, Thompson was still making occasional tours with it in 1900 when Langdon Moore became his guest.

Thompson spent his vacations at a large cottage on the shore of Swanzey Lake. He had a second cottage built about a mile away, with a long veranda that overhung the water. Like the deck of an ocean liner it provided plenty of space for exercise and it could not be seen from the highway. Back of the cottage was a fine deep well over which an attractive summer house was built, big enough for a table and a couple of chairs; and anyone who wished could sit there unobserved and plainly see and hear everyone who walked or rode along the highway.

Suddenly, without any fanfare or publicity, a tall, dignified, well-mannered man came to live in the new cottage. He poked around in the garden patch, paced back and forth on the long veranda or sat for hours in the vine-covered well house. Sometimes around sunrise he would be seen stepping into his boat practically from his bed for a few hours of early morning fishing. But he was never seen at the country store, post office or Grange hall.

It was a long time before anyone knew that this quiet man was the notorious ex-convict Langdon Moore. When it became known that he was living there at the expense of Swanzey's most respected citizen, who also furnished his food and fuel, the mystery deepened.

One of my radio listeners, William E. Nash, used to see Moore almost every day when he passed the cottage on his way to work. Sometimes he would stop and pass the time of day or exchange a word about the weather. On a few occasions Moore talked excitedly about the robberies he had committed; he confessed the crimes and seemed to be proud of them.

J. Arthur Francis of Springfield, Massachusetts, told me about the time his mother and aunt drove from Keene to Swanzey Lake for a picnic. As they started for home they saw Moore get out of his boat with an enormous pickerel. Noting their interest, he invited them to inspect his cottage: a large living room, bedroom, convenient kitchen, and everything as neat as wax. Then he offered them the fish he had just landed, which they accepted and ate that night for supper. Moore appeared to them a perfect gentleman, and when the aunt learned who he was, she said, aghast, "Isn't it terrible that such a nice old man could be so wicked!"

Mrs. John J. Veale wrote me, "When Thompson found out that folks around here were reading Moore's book, he offered to buy them up so he could destroy them, and he succeeded in getting all but a few." So that was that! And she added, "Everyone had the utmost respect for Mr. Thompson and in a country village where everyone takes you as you are, there was never too much curiosity as to why he wanted those books."

When Moore's health began to fail, his good friend Denman Thompson kept him supplied with fruit and the proper things to eat, and the housekeeper Thompson provided looked after Langdon's every want. Langdon Moore died in 1910, a year before Thompson, and both are buried in the little cemetery which is plainly in view from the old Thompson house—now a Knights of Pythias home—diagonally across the street.

I visited this burial ground not long ago. Entering by an iron gate I saw immediately the large, obelisk-like monument bearing the name THOMPSON on its base. This marks the grave of West Swanzey's most famous citizen, Denman, and his wife Maria. It dominates the little cemetery.

Walking along a wide path, I passed several rows of monuments and markers, then crossed an empty, open space. At the very back of the cemetery is the small receiving tomb, and close beside it a small square marked off with stone posts at the corners joined by iron chains. In the center of this square stands a medium-sized slab of New Hampshire granite on which is carved:

L. W. Moore

Born
May 7, 1830

Died
June 28, 1910

JOE CUSHING

ＥＶＥＲ since I told the story of
Joe Cushing's five-hundred-foot railroad in the February
1950 issue of *Reader's Digest*, I have wanted to write more
about Joe and his family—the Cushings who settled in
Hingham, Massachusetts, around 1633, and who later
founded Cushing Academy in Ashburnham.

The Cushings led active lives. They had typical pioneer
vigor and foresight. To these traits, Joseph Cushing added
a great love for horses and dogs, and a sense of fun that
was big as his own six-foot, two-hundred-pound frame.

Joe's father, Laban, grew up in Ashburnham, his parents
occupying the tavern that still stands on the old road to
Rindge, just beyond Bela Pratt's statue "The School Boy."
When Laban went over the hill to court Nancy Whitney,
the whole town knew it because he whistled and sang at
the top of his lungs. The family historian reports that
Laban was "a curly haired fellow, quick of movement and
full of fun" and that Joe's mother was a "perfect woman,

nobly planned." Laban was twenty and Nancy seventeen when they were married.

They had two daughters, and Joseph on the way, when they pulled up stakes and joined some other Ashburn-hamers who were moving to western Pennsylvania. Farm tools and furniture were loaded into one ox cart and Nancy with the two little girls in another. Laban walked between, geein', hawin', and whistlin' along the wilderness trails. At night he kept campfires going to scare off the wolves.

The Cushings reached their destination in the summer of 1817 and were warmly greeted by Laban's uncle who had preceded them and had cleared the land for a home and vegetable garden. They built a log cabin of three rooms with a loft overhead; they kept sheep and geese and hogs, and there was always hard work to be done. Like Lincoln, Joe Cushing learned his abc's by a frontier fire and at a log cabin school; everything else he learned from practical experience.

Joe brought off his first successful business venture when he was eleven and his brother Laban was eight. The two kids tapped a grove of maple trees, gathered and boiled the sap into cakes of maple sugar which Joe proudly carried to town and offered for sale. He made enough money to buy himself and his brother their very first suits of store clothes.

Two years later, the family moved back to New England and Joseph was "bound out" to a Mr. Brooks, which meant that in return for his labor Brooks would feed and clothe him and send him to school. When he should become of age, Brooks agreed to give him his freedom, a new suit and one hundred dollars in money. This was too slow a process for Joe; so he traded with Brooks and "bought his time" although he was still several years under age.

His next job was more to his liking: driving the stage-coach between Boston and Peterborough, New Hampshire. When the pony express was established between Boston and Montreal, Joe was given the Fitchburg, Massachusetts, to Keene, New Hampshire, run, and he covered the forty-four miles on horseback in four hours flat.

In Fitchburg, Joe's brother Charles ran the American House and the inevitable livery stable near by, and Joe often watched the slick "drummers" arrive from the Boston train, toss their bags into the hotel lobby and make a beeline for the stable to hire a rig and go calling on their customers. Joe made friends with these energetic salesmen and often helped them with their sample cases and the bags of grain they bought for their horses' noon-day feed.

In 1844 he opened his own grain and feed store, in a small room under the American House, and from that humble beginning came the successful J. Cushing Flour & Grain Company.

During the Civil War when many New England businesses failed, Joe Cushing prospered. The British, who favored the South, cut the telegraph line between Boston and Chicago where it ran through Canada—the telegraph which grain dealers customarily used. Besides, a man in Chicago who had a load of grain to sell wanted to be paid

in gold, not paper. Joe's solution was to travel, by train—
a two weeks' trip—to Chicago every so often, carrying
enough gold to pay for each transaction. The gold was
heavy and had to be carried in special bags which he had
made for the purpose.

Sometimes he would drive up to Canada with a bag of
gold on the seat with him and purchase the heavy Perch-
erons which were raised in Sherbrooke. When he returned,
he'd have a string of fine horses behind his buggy.

Joe also dabbled in lumber and real estate, and he was
never happier than when he got in his top buggy to go
rattling off to appraise a piece of farm land or a wood lot,
his tiny fox terrier beside him and a great mastiff loping
along behind. Most men, going into the woods to inspect
a "heater piece" would have left their horse and carriage
by the side of the road and walked in—but not Joe Cushing!
He drove right through the farmer's tall timothy, or sometimes up to his hubs in mud and water, the alders and
hackmatack brushing the buggy, till finally his horse's nose
was smack up against a spruce tree and turning around a
physical impossibility. When he had sized up the property,
he would unharness, turn the horse, then lift and swing
the buggy around, harness up again, climb aboard and
drive lickety-split back to town.

They said around Fitchburg, "Joe Cushing's smarter
than chain lightnin', but he's straight as a yard of pump
water."

So Joe continued to prosper. And, needing larger quarters, in 1868 he cast an appraising eye on Fitchburg's most

prominent landmark—the Old Stone Mill which stood like a fortress on the bank of the Nashua River. The great granite blocks that formed its walls had not been "histed" into place by steam derrick, but dragged up an earthern ramp by ox team. Old-timers could remember how strange the long-horned steers had looked, peering patiently over the third story stonework like a battery of bovine sentinels.

Joe admired the magnificent water wheel, the twelve-by-twelve timbers, and the faded wooden tablet that proclaimed, "On this spot, on the morning of April 17th, 1775, the Minute Men of Fitchburg met and marched to Lexington."

So he purchased the Old Stone Mill, and made a number of additions, among them a towering grain elevator that seemed to reach to the sky, and a spur track which reached to the Boston and Maine Railroad. Grain for the Cushing mill was unloaded from freight cars and the B&M siding onto one of Joe's boxcars; two matched pairs of oxen with satin-smooth hides and upsweeping horns pulled it slowly over the new spur track, and when the grain had been ground, the ox teams hauled it back.

It is interesting to note that the first freight train to pass through the Hoosac Tunnel in 1875 carried a load of grain consigned to Joe Cushing's mill in Fitchburg. And that the electric locomotive used after the oxen were sold was the first ever built by the General Electric Co. and was exhibited at the Chicago World's Fair.

But it was the five-hundred-foot spur track over which the oxen dragged the boxcars that brought fame to Joe

Cushing. When this was completed,* Joe said to his son: "Milton, we ought to have a dedication, the way the Union Pacific did a couple of years ago." He hired the local printer to get out some classy invitations that read in part:

GRAND SPIKE DRIVING AND OPENING CEREMONIES OF THE JOE CUSHING RAILROAD, FITCHBURG, MASS.

You are cordially invited to be present at the Driving of the Last Spike and to attend the Formal Opening of this new Railroad on Saturday evening, September 2nd, 1871. A SPECIAL TRAIN will leave Fitchburg Depot at 8 P.M., passing over the new road and arriving at Cushing Station, its Western Terminus, on time.

A great crowd turned out on that warm September night and shortly before eight o'clock a B&M locomotive coupled into flag-draped flatcars with settees for the local notables. The Fitchburg Cornet Band struck up "Yankee Doodle," the engineer tooted the whistle, and off they went over 500 feet of Joe Cushing's iron rails.

The Special halted and police opened a passageway in the crowd so the headlight could shine upon the track for the Spike Driving Ceremony. With great dignity, Joe removed his resplendent cutaway coat and tall silk hat, and solemnly drove a freshly gilded pine spike into the cinders beside the track. The band blared, the crowd cheered, and the red fire smoked and spluttered.

* The following material reprinted by kind permission of *The Reader's Digest.*

During the speeches that followed, one orator shouted: "The driving of this gold spike is a milestone in American railroading." A local wag nudged his neighbor and whispered: "Don't he mean the tenth of a milestone?"

It was way past ten o'clock when they cleaned up platters of cold meats, several large cheeses, a keg of sour pickles and gallons of rum. And from that moment on the spur track was "The Joe Cushing Railroad."

Next Joe ordered some stationery, a two-color job on bond paper. Superimposed on a fine engraving of the Old Stone Mill, with freight cars out front, was "The Joe Cushing Railroad" in heavy Old English. At the left of the letterhead the Board of Directors were listed, and at the right was "J. Cushing, Supt."

Then Joe had some fancy passes printed, and signed them with a Spencerian flourish. When things were dull at the mill he would dash off letters to the presidents of the nation's big railroads. The letters went something like this:

Dear Sir:

It is my belief that in this rapidly growing country of ours the railroads play an important part in binding the land together. To further this spirit I am presenting you, on behalf of the Cushing Railroad, a complimentary Pass which will permit you to travel at will over our entire system. I hope that if you are ever in New England you will avail yourself of this opportunity and enjoy our hospitality.

Yours faithfully, etc.

Not to be outdone by a jerkwater road, the big railroads reciprocated and, before the year ended, Joe had enough passes to enable him to travel all over the country.

And then came the day!

Into the yard of J. CUSHING & CO. ("FLOUR & GRAIN") there stalked, one hot summer morning, an important-appearing gentleman with striped pants, mutton-chop whiskers, gold-headed cane—and one of Joe's passes. He was the president of a big western railroad who had been pleased to receive the superintendent's cordial letter. Being in New England, he had come to Fitchburg to ride on the Cushing Railroad.

Joe politely asked the stranger if he had time to ride over *all* the system. The visitor pursed his lips and said, well, he had two days to spend. Whereupon Joe called to his assistant who was sorting grain bags on the platform: "Have the President's car made ready! And clear the track for a special run!"

A few minutes later, the dumfounded visitor was personally assisted by Supt. Cushing onto a flag-festooned flatcar and seated in a broken-down barber's chair. Behind it was one of those old-fashioned orange-and-black advertising umbrellas, and to one side was a big brass cuspidor.

A yoke of long-horned oxen had been backed into place and chained to the flatcar. Joe gee'd the off ox, goaded the nigh one, and the Cushing Special, its sole passenger a bug-eyed executive of one of the most important railroads in the country, went rolling off along the 500-foot spur.

When they reached the end of the line Joe said sheepishly: "I hope you are not insulted by my little joke. I know this isn't much of a railroad. But it's mine, and I'm proud of it."

"Insulted? I should say not! This is the best Yankee trick I ever heard of. Just wait till I get back home and urge all my railroad friends to use their passes on the Cushing Railroad in Fitchburg!"

He held out his hand, and the two men shook and shook, and then shook with laughter over Joe Cushing's joke.

TWO WANDERERS*

Some three or four miles west of Rindge Center, New Hampshire, there used to be a little community of farm houses scattered along a lonely country road. Near by was a swamp with a small stream and an old mill with a water wheel; if you don't mind getting your feet wet and your clothes scratched by briers, you can still see the rusted machinery of that mill up there today.

Overlooking the road and the swamp was a high, grassy knoll on which stood a weather-beaten, forlorn-looking house, gray and gaunt against the winter sky. I shall always regret that I did not go to Rindge when I first heard this story, but like a good many other things, I put it off until too late. I delayed until after the house had been torn down, but I did find some of the timbers, the cellar walls and an old well partially filled with water.

As near as I can find out, it was late in the fall of 1816 when the first of a series of unusual happenings took place

* Reprinted by kind permission of *Yankee Magazine*.

there. On a raw November night, when black clouds hung low over Monadnock, already sprinkled with snow, the folks who lived in the house on the knoll heard a loud knock on their front door. The farmer grabbed a candle, unbolted the door and peered at a tired-looking young man in his early twenties.

"My name is John Smith," he said through chattering teeth. "I got lost in the swamp; then I saw your light, and I wonder if you could put me up for the night?"

"Why I guess we can take care of a traveler, can't we, Ma?"

And she said, "Of course! He can have the front room. But come into the kitchen, boy, and get warm."

Mr. Smith was carrying a box which he placed on the floor, and then sank wearily into a rocking chair. He ate apple pie and drank tea, and with a polite "Thank you, ma'am" he took two warm blankets and rolled up on the couch in the front room. In no time, he was sound asleep.

When the farmer arose in the morning, he found that John Smith had already filled the wood box, fetched water from the well and washed up at the sink.

"I'm not much good at milking cows, sir, but I can swing an ax, and if you could use a man for his board and room, I'd like to stay on a spell."

"Fair enough, son! Fair enough! You can help me fix my fence. Ever try yanking out willer stumps?"

John Smith gave a good, honest, hard day's work for his food and shelter, and every night after supper he would take his candle, retreat into his room, and close the door.

The farmer and his wife often stayed up till nine-thirty or so, she sewing or reading her Bible, he smoking his pipe and getting up now and then to toss chunks of apple wood into the fireplace. They could see the sliver of light under the door across the hall, and they often spoke about John, wondering where he came from and speculating on the contents of the box that was his only luggage.

One night after supper, instead of going directly to his chamber, Smith said, "I've been looking at the bare walls of your front room, and I was wondering if you'd mind if I did a little decorating? It's quite the style these days to have flowers and things painted on plaster walls. Brightens the room up quite a bit."

"That will be lovely, Mr. Smith! Won't it, Pa?"

Pa said it was all right with him, too. "Go right ahead, son. Paint anything you want. You'll find some brushes out in the barn."

But Smith said eagerly, "Oh, I brought my own brushes and dry colors. I do think I ought to mix them down cellar, though. Grinding paint would dirty up the house."

So that was what he had in the box, paints and brushes!

Well, the first stormy day that kept the men inside, Smith pounded and mixed his colors and put them up in papers, and after supper, with three candles on the fireplace mantel and two more on the table, he began to work. Standing on a box, he traced with a piece of charcoal the delicate outlines of the murals which later caused a sensation in Rindge, New Hampshire.

Insisting that the farmer and his wife should not look at

the paintings until he had finished, the artist kept the door locked, even making up his own bed, and night after night, he worked long after the old folks had gone to sleep. Sometimes they'd waken enough to hear him tiptoe up or down the cellar stairs.

As I said, I did not go to Rindge in time to see the paintings that John Smith left, but many folks did see them, and I know a little about them. In style they were primitive; in color they were brilliant, with strong, clear shades of red, blue and green. They were pastoral scenes mostly, but one whole wall was given over to coastal scenes: old wharves with sailboats, fish houses and lobster pots.

It took Smith several weeks to decorate all four walls and the ceiling of the front room, and it was well into February when he finished. It had been storming for two whole days. The roads were blocked and the snow had drifted way up over the fence posts. It cleared off cold with a flaming red sunset, and the night wind whipped up the fine, dry snow and sent it spiraling like smoke. The mercury dropped to twenty below.

It was so cold that night, the farmer pulled his chair close to the fire, and between cat naps stoked it to keep it going briskly. About midnight, his wife fished hot bricks from the hearth and wrapped them in flannel to take to bed, and then she noticed the crack of light under the door across the hall.

Tapping her husband's shoulder, she said, "Ask John if he would like a hot brick and a cup of tea. He must be frozen."

The old man got up and rapped lightly on the door.
"John!"

There was no answer. "Humph! Guess he's fallen
asleep."

He rapped louder. "John! Mother's made some tea.
Come out and have some."

Only the whine of the snow-laden wind and the soft
singing of the tea kettle broke the silence. He rattled the
door but it was fastened. Putting his shoulder against it,
he pushed, and almost fell in as the latch came off and
clattered to the floor.

"Mother! Come quick! Looka here!"

The two old folks stood there, staring at the strange,
colorful room, at big red barns behind tiny white farm
houses, and covered bridges, and church steeples rising
above rolling green fields, and cows, horses and sheep. An
empty room, for John Smith had vanished! On the mantel-
piece was his brush still wet with paint, and under it on one
side of the fireplace were these words: "This room painted
by J. Smith 1817."

They went over every inch of the house, from cellar to
garret; there was no one there but themselves. They
stayed up all night, thinking John Smith might come back,
and when daylight came they put on their snowshoes and
walked all around the house, but not a footprint did they
find in the freshly drifted snow.

I called on several persons in Rindge who had been
familiar with the mysterious house. When Mrs. Harris
Rice was a little girl, she used to visit the house on the knoll

to play with the children who lived there. Sometimes she stayed overnight. Lying in bed in the front chamber, the young visitor would look around the room at the bright pictures. Gazing upward to the ceiling, she would study the rosettes and streamers of an ornate, Italian-style medallion. And over the dummy fireplace were vases of flowers so vivid she imagined she could grasp them.

Mr. Henry Hale had his own theory about Smith's disappearance. He said, "When I investigated that house many years ago, I found a secret chamber in back of the chimney. It was narrow and dark, but I squeezed in, and climbed up, and I came out in a tiny hidden space under the eaves. There was not room to stand, but a man could sit there or lie down. And I also found that the outside clapboards covered a cleverly made trap door which fitted so tightly you would never guess it was there, and after being opened it would fall back into place."

Mr. Hale believed that Smith used this upstairs door to drop into the snow where his tracks would be covered rapidly on a wild night like that. And, by the way, Mr. Hale had seen Smith's signature on the panel of the fireplace "many times."

And now we come to the final episode.

Several weeks after Smith disappeared, two strangers called at the house and asked a lot of questions. They admitted they were detectives and wanted to look at the paintings, carefully comparing the signature with some papers they had.

The farmer asked, "What do you want of John Smith? Has he committed a crime?"

"No," they said, "but he thinks he did. You see," the detective went on, "this John Smith was a temperamental young fellow subject to spells of depression. When he was feeling low, he'd take a drink and he wasn't a man who could handle his liquor. One night at a party, he got into an argument with a pal of his who was playing up to Smith's young lady friend. They had some words, and all of a sudden Smith picked up a stove poker and struck his friend, causing him to fall and bang his head on the andiron. Thinking he had killed him, Smith dashed out of the house and ran away. It's taken us a long time to trace him this far."

And the second detective added, "Actually, the chap wasn't hurt bad at all. He's the one who's paying us to look for Smith and tell him to come back."

As far as I know, John Smith never did go back and there is no record of his travels after that, unless he left his mark by painting some of the murals "by an unknown artist" still to be seen on the plastered walls of old New England houses.

II

Rambling 'round New England as I have for the past quarter century, with camera, notebook and an insatiable curiosity, I have come across some mighty interesting anecdotes concerning the odd and interesting characters who used to be familiar figures on the highways and byways.

Usually, they traveled on foot and alone unless accompanied by a dog. If they were not invited to curl up in the hay, or sleep in the shed, they'd find a comfortable spot alongside the stone wall, or under a tree and with leaves for a blanket, they'd snooze thru the starry night. Only when a line storm or freezing blizzard raged would they ever consent to occupy the bliss of a feather bed inside the farmhouse.

If one of these itinerant travelers did condescend to have supper with the family, then curl up on the living room couch, you can be sure his every move and word was remembered and talked about, for many moons thereafter.

A classic example of this type of "tramp" was old Cling Clang, tin knocker and clock fixer who frequented the coastal towns of Maine, sometimes jumped over into New Hampshire and once every few seasons, larruped up into King's County, Nova Scotia. It was there, about 75 years ago, that Cling Clang sought shelter under the hospitable roof of Daniel Sanford, providing unexpected entertainment for the big family of boys and girls. Mrs. Sanford made the kids eat first, then packed them off upstairs to bed. For the next hour, they lay on their tummies, pressing close to the cracks in the floor boards to watch Cling Clang eat the first good-sized meal he'd had in weeks. One of the girls, now Emily Sanford Henniker, tells me: "My dad and uncles still talk about old Cling Clang. They never forgot how they spied on him through the cracks of the ceiling and watched him eat. Always, he finished one part of his meal before tackling another. First, he'd eat all of his potato, then his squash or onions. Then he'd eat several biscuits, or slices of bread, then eat the butter and lap up the gravy. Never did he mix them. I've seen him drink his tea, straight and clear and then eat two spoonfuls of sugar."

After he'd satisfied his hunger, Cling Clang would reach in the enormous bag he carried over his back and fish out a well-worn and unpainted barrel head. He used this as a cushion, while he sat and worked on the clocks and every night of his life it became his pillow. When he was asked to sleep in the main house, where it was warm beside the coal stove, he'd shake his long hair and point to the shed, and out there he would go with his barrel head for a pillow and curl up in a corner, where it was nice and cool. They say he brought that barrel head from Europe, and once it was under him, he'd sleep like a log. But—he was always up and gone before the crack of dawn next morning.

When he stopped over at farm houses he would always ask the farmer if there was a rooster on the place and if told "Yes" he would look distracted, then say, plaintively, "Would you put a basket over him, so he won't crow in the morning?" For some strange reason, the crowing of a rooster and the crying of a baby so completely upset Cling Clang he'd go almost out of his mind.

All over Hancock county, Maine, there are farm folks who remember his allergy to crowing roosters, and when the clock fixer stopped one night at Swan's Island, some mischievous boys let their Plymouth Rock rooster loose, about 4 A.M. and he crowed lustily. Cling Clang dashed out of the shed, bag and barrel head hugged close to him, and mounting his poles went leaping down the road, screaming as if in pain. He was never seen at Swan's Island again.

I first heard of this odd character from "Chief" Stanwood, who runs the Big Chief hunting camps at Tunk Lake in East Sullivan, Maine. He was just a boy when Cling Clang covered the country but he remembers seeing him as he "poled" it down the long hill in Ellsworth. He had two, long, brass-tipped poles and by grasping them as high as he could reach, he could leap ahead, ten to twelve feet at a bound, and in this way he could cover the country six or seven miles an hour. Swinging over fences and ditches was easy for Cling.

As he carried all his equipment, as well as new pots and pans, in the bags on his back, they naturally rattled and banged when he leaped, giving him the nickname of Old Cling Clang. He could be heard coming a half a mile away but when he saw a horse and team, he leaped to the side of the road and remained quiet until the team had passed.

Cling never wore civilized clothing. He made his own suits out of the bags and old gunny sacks he found lying around the salt ships and freight sheds. They were awesome looking clothes but serviceable. On his head he wore nothing except a thick shock of gray hair, which being long, trailed after his head like a veil, when he was going full tilt. He always went barefoot until the snow came; then he fashioned pieces of bags into funny-looking footwear. These, and his socks, shirt and suit, he washed out every three or four days, regardless of the weather. There are folks living in New England today who can remember seeing this strange character doing his laundry, on the ledges near Trenton, Maine, when the temperature was down below zero. When he had a blanket or bedding with him, he always washed it in salt water and spread it on a bush to dry.

One winter's day, after Cling Clang had been seen in Sullivan, going from house to house with his tin ware, he was suddenly missed. Somebody said, "You don't s'pose he's sick or something? Maybe he's asleep under that over-turned boat." Well, they went down and looked and there was poor old Cling Clang, his steel-like fingers frozen in death to his beloved barrel head. The town of Sullivan buried the queer, pole-jumping character, but I can't say just where, for all the records were burned up.

A lot of strange hermits and tramps have traveled the highways and byways of New England, but none more strange than old Cling Clang.

VISIONS AND
HOODOOED SHIPS

THE 1400-ton square rigger
N. T. Hill was launched from the Ginn Yard, Bucksport,
Maine, in June 1876. As it was customary to name a new
ship for the heaviest stockholder, this one was named for
Nahun Train Hill, a Yankee big shot of Bucksport when
that upriver town was in its heyday.

Nahun Hill owned shares in several ships; he also dabbled
in real estate, and they still tell of the fuss he caused when
he painted his big house at the corner of Main and Mechanic
streets. Most houses in Bucksport then were traditionally
white, with dark green blinds, but Hill, having on hand a
consignment of yellowish-brown paint which he couldn't
sell, applied it to the big, square house with devastating
effect. The pastor of the Congregational Church, which
was near by, asked, "Why didn't you make your house
white, Mr. Hill?" To which Nahun snapped, "If I choose
to paint my house the color of tobacco juice, that's my

privilege, and nobody else's business," and added, "It's time that paint was used!"

When the ship *N. T. Hill* neared completion, the owners were undecided which of the local seafaring men should be her captain. They argued for days, and finally put it up to Nahun Hill. He came out strongly for his lifelong friend, Captain Jabez Snow, a veteran of many years' sailing on the seven seas.

"I know he's getting old, but he's a good man. He's never lost a ship, and his voyages have always paid well. With him in command, we won't need to put on much insurance." The other stockholders agreed.

When told he was their first choice, Jabez rubbed his chin and said thoughtfully, "It's kind of you to ask me, but I was figurin' on stayin' ashore. There's several things I want to do before I git too old. However, I guess they can wait. All right, I'll take it, but this will positively be my last voyage!"

When I went to Bucksport to get this and other stories, I stopped at the old Jed Prouty Tavern where I happened to run into Henry Buxton, then feature writer for the Bangor *Daily News*. I told him I was getting dope on the *N. T. Hill* for a broadcast, and he said, "Oh, the hoodooed ship! Did you ever hear what happened the day she was launched? I got the story straight from Ambrose H. White, vice-president of the International Paper Company."

I had not heard this one, so Buxton gave me the details.

It seems that when Ambrose White was just a little shaver, his father took him to the Ginn shipyard to see the launching of the *N. T. Hill.* To keep the big ship in midstream, several stout cables had been strung from the *N. T. Hill,* still on the stocks, to trees along the river bank, and one of the cables was fastened securely to the oak tree under which the Whites were seated. For some reason, Ambrose became frightened and wanted to move, so his father agreeably took him to a different vantage point. It was lucky he did, for when the *N. T. Hill* started to slide, the cable became taut, smoked, and then snapped with the sound of a gun as the old oak tree splintered into a shower of rotten wood and slivers, the biggest branch crashing to the ground where the Whites had been sitting.

I hadn't known of the Whites' narrow escape, but I did know that the *N. T. Hill,* freed of one of her guiding lines, veered sharply to starboard, shoving her bow into the mud flats of Verona Island.

Another mishap occurred while the *N. T. Hill* was being towed to the wharf for her final rigging. Captain Jabez Snow, a stickler for having things shipshape, noticed that one of the flags had fouled around the mainmast, so he shouted for someone to "go aloft and shake out that ensign." A workman sprang into the rigging, freed the flag, and was about to come down when he either slipped or became dizzy—anyway the crowd on shore was horrified to see him suddenly pitch forward and fall to the deck.

When the ship docked, the injured man was rushed to a hospital. He was still there when the *N. T. Hill* set sail for Liverpool.

Naturally, such mishaps coming in quick succession had

a dampening effect on the spirits of everyone—for a ship that had an accident during launching was a bad-luck ship. But things like that rolled off the broad back of Captain Jabez Snow like water off a seagull. His only trouble was domestic.

As I got the story, Mrs. Snow, for reasons not given, puffed up the stairs to her attorney's office, and announced tartly, "I want a divorce!" Quite surprised, the lawyer wheezed amiably, "Now don't start dragging your anchor, ma'am. Captain Jabez is going on a long voyage. Just rest on your oars a spell; maybe you won't have to divorce him." And as it worked out, she didn't.

Before this, Captain Snow had never had any trouble getting a ship's crew, but because of the superstitions and hard-luck rumors which spread about the *N. T. Hill*, only a handful of local men signed up for her maiden voyage. Captain Snow was disgusted with all the idle talk. "Hoo-dooed, my eye!" he snorted. "She's as fine a ship as ever sailed. If they don't want to sail with Snow as master— I'll get a crew from New York or Boston!"

A few days before the *N. T. Hill* was scheduled to sail, the crew arrived in Bucksport—as rough and tough a gang of ill-assorted "furriners" as ever were dragged from the dives and brothels of New York's waterfront. Hardly one knew who he was or where he was going. A few managed to stagger aboard the spanking new ship, but most were literally lugged over the side and dumped into the fo'castle bunks.

Captain Snow smiled with satisfaction. Nahun T. Hill and everyone else in Bucksport feared the worst.

Well, they sailed, but they had been out only a few hours when the third accident occurred. It had been breezing on steadily and Captain Snow was making the most of the wind, wholly unconcerned as great green waves towered above the deck, then smashed across it. One of those huge waves broke on the bow and engulfed the Gilley boy from Bucksport. He was knocked down, then swept over the side into the churning sea. Captain Snow knew the boy and liked him, but with the wind blowing half a gale, he feared he'd strip his spars if he tried to wear around. He swallowed hard, shut his ears to the faint cries from the water, and kept right on his course.

The loss of this local boy had a pronounced effect on the rest of the already demoralized crew. They now firmly believed they were on a jinxed ship, and their captain, they figured, was a hardhearted master whose only thought was to make a record run and earn a lot of money for the owners. From now on the slightest, commonplace occurrence was magnified out of all proportion. An overturned hatch cover, a broken mirror, the appearance of St. Elmo's fire at the masthead, threw them into a panic. In spite of their feelings, they did make Liverpool safe and sound, and lost no time in dashing to the nearest saloon to drown their apprehension.

Captain Jabez remained as cool as a cucumber. While the *N. T. Hill* was in Liverpool, he had her ironed and loaded with a cargo of coal. Then, with almost a new crew, he sailed to Rangoon where he scouted around for a return cargo that would bring his owners, back in Bucksport, a good profit and himself a fine bonus.

With his Yankee instinct for finding out things, Captain Snow learned that a bumper crop of rice would be harvested that year; so he went inland and bought heavily. His plan was to make a quick run back to the States before some other captain got the same idea. While he waited for the rice to be brought to the dock side, Jabez ordered the *N. T. Hill* overhauled and cleaned till she was as spic and span as his kitchen back in Maine. Then, when the last trace of coal had been removed, ton upon ton of gleaming rice was stowed aboard until the ship was loaded eighteen inches above the Plimsoll mark!

The *N. T. Hill* cast off early in January 1877, headed for New York.

In Brewer, Maine, a scant twenty miles above Bucksport, Zenas Lawry was suddenly awakened one stormy morning that January, by a cry of "Help!" He peered sleepily from his warm blankets and saw, standing by the foot of his bed, the forlorn and wet figure of his next-door neighbor, Ephraim Thurston. Ephraim was only partially dressed and had a blanket wrapped around his shoulders. Zenas Lawry noted that his friend's face was deathly pale and the hand which rested on the footboard of his bed was blue with cold and glistening wet.

Zenas, now fully awake, gasped, "What's the trouble, Ephraim?" And at that, the vision, or whatever it was, faded from sight. Only the sound of wind broke the early morning silence.

Zenas jumped out of bed, hurriedly dressed and went down-stairs. He shook down the coal stove, opened the draft and raised the living-room shades. Down the street a way he could see Thurston's house, but there was no sign of anyone's being up.

At breakfast, Zenas announced that he had seen Ephraim Thurston that morning; but his family just laughed. His wife said, "Forget it and drink your coffee. You had a dawn-dream; they're always more vivid than a nightmare."

Zenas banged the table. "I wasn't dreaming! I was wide awake! I tell you I saw Ephraim Thurston standing at the foot of my bed! He was wringing wet and called for help!"

"But he couldn't have," his daughter protested. "Have you forgotten that Ephraim sailed last year with Captain Snow on the *N. T. Hill?*"

"Then she must have come in!" said Zenas.

But she had not come in. January passed, then February and March. In the early spring a clipper brought word that the *N. T. Hill* had been seen in Rangoon the previous December and must have sailed soon after. Summer came, and fall. No vessel reported having sighted the *Hill,* and the owners had to assume she was lost. To the very last Nahun T. Hill believed that Captain Snow would come through with flying colors. But after a year had gone by with no word, he closed his books with this notation:

"*N. T. Hill.* Sailed from Rangoon January 1877. Long overdue and presumably lost at sea with all hands."

Talking with the late Lincoln Colcord, noted marine authority of Searsport, Maine, I asked what he thought happened to the *N. T. Hill.*

"I think I can solve that one!" Colcord said. "In all probability the rice got wet, swelled, and sprung the timbers. I checked up, and found that a typhoon swept the Bay of Bengal right after the *Hill* sailed."

That would have been approximately the time the vision of Ephraim Thurston appeared to Zenas Lawry!

II

While Captain Leander Foss was directing the final work on his new bark *Isadore*, up in Kennebunk, Maine, he called to one of the carpenters. "How'd you like to make the maiden trip with us, Mr. King? It won't take very long and you can pick up a few extra dollars. Think it over and let me know."

Thomas King thought it would be fun to make a quick trip to New Orleans, and as his wife said they could certainly use the money, he signed on as a member of the crew, receiving a month's wages in advance.

That night, King had a very disturbing nightmare: he saw seven coffins lying side by side on the Kennebunk wharf!

A big crowd came down to the shore the day the *Isadore* was to be launched. But something went wrong. She shivered, shook, and then fetched up short right in the middle of the ways. Old-timers shook their heads and mumbled, "It's a bad sign! Ships that stick when launching always run into trouble!"

At high tide the following day, the 400-ton vessel was started again. Instead of gliding gracefully into the water, the *Isadore* wavered and careened so the crowd feared she was going to capsize. She was launched after a fashion, and towed to Kennebunkport to be rigged, ballasted and loaded for her maiden voyage.

Again, that night, Thomas King dreamed of the seven coffins, and this time the long, black boxes bore names of the *Isadore's* crew. He was looking for his own name when he woke up in a cold sweat, so scared he couldn't get back to sleep.

His wife demanded to know what was bothering him; so he told her about the nightmares, and for quite a while they discussed the matter, back and forth: should he make the voyage, or should he consider that he had a warning not to sail? Finally, King said, "I can't back out now. I've signed my papers, and accepted my pay and I won't be a quitter."

The night before the *Isadore* was scheduled to sail, Thomas King dreamed about the caskets for a third time, and he heard a voice say, "One of them is for you!"

That settled it! Bright and early, he went to the wharf and handed Captain Foss his wages, saying, "I've changed my mind. I don't want to go on this voyage. Get someone to take my place."

Captain Foss was furious. "You know I can't get any-body this late! We sail on the next tide. Get your duffel aboard, and be quick about it!"

Without another word, King turned and ran from the wharf as fast as he could, disappearing into the near-by woods. He did not see the *Isadore* sail on the high tide at noon.

She made a handsome picture as she got under way, her new white sails sparkling in the late November sunshine. Captain Foss was jubilant as he waved good-by, but the sailors were glum and downcast as the water widened be-tween the bark and her native shore.

One member of the crew, who lived two miles inland, was so reluctant to leave his family that he didn't reach the wharf until the *Isadore* had started. He was about to return home when a friend hailed him. "Toss your bag in my dory. I'll set ye aboard." All the way out, the sailor kept silent. Turning half around, he sat looking at the familiar skyline as if he knew he would never see it again. When they reached the side of the almost motionless ship, the man said, "You came near missing your passage." And the sailor replied, "I wish I had."

Back on shore, the townspeople watched the *Isadore* drift down the bay, her white sails outlined against a lemon-colored sky. There was no wind and the sea was like glass. Distant islands appeared to be upside down, a phenomenon that always meant a change in the weather.

It came quite suddenly. Low black clouds scudded across

the horizon and spread rapidly with a freshening breeze. The breeze turned into a gale that brought sleet, then heavy snow that blotted out the bark *Isadore* and sent the watchers scurrying to their homes.

Weekly prayer meeting, held that night in spite of the storm, was attended by many of the families of the men who had sailed on the *Isadore*. They sang the old familiar hymns and joined in prayers offered by the parson for all their men at sea. Outside, the wind-driven snow piled up in drifts, and ice-laden branches crackled overhead.

After the meeting, a few neighbors lingered around the potbellied stove. The chief topic of conversation was the *Isadore*. One woman said, "My John was awful upset. I've never seen him cry before. When it came time to go, he hugged me hard and made me promise to take care of the children." Another woman spoke up. "George was scairt too. He had a bad dream last week. Said he dreamed the ship went on the rocks and all of them were pitched into the sea."

And so it went, until it was clear that every single member of the crew had received some "warning" not to sail!

With heavy hearts, the little group pushed into the storm and struck out through the drifts for their individual homes.

By noon next day, the weather had cleared, and a bright sun sparkled on trees and fields. Men came with ox teams and shovels to break out the roads. Women went to the general store, the kids played in the snow. And a few miles away, at York, where the surf was pounding against Bald Head cliff, a great mass of wreckage was coming ashore— the smashed and broken timbers of a proud new ship!

Shortly after noon, a man reached Kennebunkport with the news. "*Isadore* shipwrecked at Bald Head! All smashed to pieces! Not a soul saved!"

All Kennebunkport went into mourning. At the Baptist Church, parishioners gathered again to console each other and to pray. Mrs. Thomas King was among them, for she had not seen her husband since he left the house for his interview with Captain Foss.

Fifteen local men had sailed on the bark *Isadore*, but only seven bodies were pulled out of the wreckage that floated around the rocky base of Bald Head. When they were all accounted for, there were seven black coffins on the wharf, just as Thomas King had seen them in his dream. But there was none for him.

Two days after the shipwreck, a tired, shivering man staggered out of the woods at twilight. Making his way to the home of "Widow" King, he knocked on the door. When Mrs. King opened it, she screamed, "Thomas! God be praised! You escaped the wreck!"

Then Thomas confessed that he had not sailed on the *Isadore*. He had spent two nights in the woods, hiding in a camp until driven home by hunger.

Thomas tried to make himself out a coward for deserting the *Isadore* at the last moment, but to his wife and friends he was a hero. And the parson expressed all their feelings when he added, "Thomas King heard God's warning and heeded it!"

Thomas continued to work in the shipyard at Kenne-bunkport for a while, then left Maine for good. In the last years of his life, he lived in Boston and worked at the Charlestown navy yard. One day in 1865, just after he had passed his sixty-fifth birthday, King handed out cigars to his fellow workers. He grinned happily.

"We've got a new baby boy at our house. I'm naming him David, and I hope he'll make a good man for Uncle Sam's navy!"

When David King was seventeen years old, he did join the navy, and sailed away to the Far East. It was while the squadron was in China that his aged father passed away, and David, feeling lonely talked to his shipmates about Thomas King. One of them said suddenly, "Why—that's the name of the survivor of the bark *Isadore!* Was he *that* Thomas King?"

"I dunno," said David. "That was his name, but I never heard him say anything about the *Isadore.*"

The sailor told him about the shipwreck, and when he mentioned Kennebunkport, David cried, "My father used to live up there!"

After serving his hitch in the navy, David returned to Boston and went to work for the Boston & Maine Railroad. When I talked to him in 1946, he had retired and was living in Holliston, Massachusetts. We sat on his big veranda and he told me the most surprising part of this story.

"It was very strange," he said slowly. "In 1897 I was working for the B & M over in East Boston. As I started across the yard one day pushing a wheelbarrow, a gust of wind scattered a bundle of old papers and rubbish I was planning to burn in the incinerator. One of the flying pieces landed face up on my coat sleeve, and the wind held it there long enough for me to read: *The Ill-fated Isadore.*

"I grabbed it quick! There was a footnote that gave the names of the crew including my father. It said, 'Thomas King also shipped, but ran away before the vessel sailed.' It was the first page of some kind of pamphlet, but that's all there was . . . just the front page."

David King told me he hunted all over the freight yard, looking at every piece of paper he came across. He poked around the ties and under the platforms, and raked through every pile of rubbish. At the end of three weeks, he had all the missing pages of a small pamphlet advertising Mitchell's Original Belladonna Plasters! He stuck them together and there, in print, he had the story of the shipwreck of the bark *Isadore*, and Thomas King's fateful dream!

SIDE SHOWS

Here in New England
people will never forget Phineas T. Barnum, not only because of his connection with "The Greatest Show on
Earth," but because he discovered the Swedish Nightin-
gale, Jenny Lind; the two New England midgets, General
and Mrs. Tom Thumb; and the giant elephant Jumbo.

These worldwide attractions were real, not faked in any
way. Other attractions, which were not what they seemed,
Barnum fooled the public into enjoying because he could
take anything and produce a show out of it.

Born in Bethel, Connecticut, in 1810, Phineas was taught
to do chores like any other country boy. He drove cows,
weeded the garden, split wood, and as soon as he was old
enough to wait on customers, he went to clerk in Deacon
Smith's corner grocery store.

Here he got a "strict" religious and business bringing-up.
Each Monday morning Deacon Smith would arrive at the
store and peer over his glasses to see if Phineas had swept
up and had filled the woodbox. Then he would ask, "Boy,

did you remember to put water in the rum, and dust in the pepper box?"

"Yes, sir!"

"Did you mix chicory with the coffee?"

"Yes I did, Deacon."

"Well, that's fine. Now come upstairs and we'll say our morning prayers."

While it isn't generally known, Phineas T. Barnum knew the Bible backward and forward, and it was at a prayer meeting that he met the girl whom he married. After their first son was born, they moved to New York.

Waiting his turn in a barber shop one day, Barnum overheard a man describe the aged colored woman who was being exhibited in Philadelphia as Joyce Heth, the slave who took care of George Washington. "Just think!" said the man. "She was present when the Father of our country was born! Next month she'll be one hundred-sixty years old!"

Phineas dashed home, borrowed train fare to Philadelphia, and went at once to see Joyce Heth. She was toothless and nearly blind but she still sucked on an old clay pipe. She showed a yellowing bill of sale stating that Augustine Washington, George's father, had sold his slave, Joyce Heth, for thirty-three pounds lawful money.

Phineas made her an offer and wound up as owner and manager of George Washington's colored nurse. Press notices which he prepared for the newspapers were printed, read and generally believed. But in Boston, where Barnum exhibited Joyce Heth in an empty store, some folks were skeptical. "She's nothing but a rubber-faced dummy," a Boston paper claimed, "worked by wires while her squeaky voice comes from a clever ventriloquist behind the curtains." Barnum denied this charge in half-page newspaper ads, and folks came to see her until Joyce Heth suddenly died. After an autopsy, medical authorities reported that the "so-called Joyce Heth" was only seventy years old and obviously a fake. The press lambasted Barnum for playing such a hoax but he had learned a valuable lesson: the public liked freaks and would pay to see them.

Barnum began hiring all sorts of strange characters for his tent shows: thin men, fat girls, strong guys, and folks with elastic skin. When natural curiosities were scarce, he invented them. There was, for instance, the horse that my Uncle Charley used to chuckle over, "with its head where its tail ought to be." This was a real horse all right, and Barnum had simply *backed* him into the stall so that literally his head was where his tail should have been.

When P. T. Barnum bought Scudder's American Museum in New York City, he had to show something new every two weeks and that kept him busy and on his toes. He went in for "spectaculars" and his first show of this kind was "Niagara Falls in all its glory" complete with running water. By means of handbills, posters and ads in country papers, couples who could not afford to spend their honeymoons at the real Falls were urged to come to New York to see the faithful replica. They came by the thousands.

A serious drought was on and there had been several

disastrous fires, so the New York Water Commission figured that Mr. Barnum was using more water than he should, and that he had better shut down Niagara Falls until water was plentiful again. Barnum's reply was a cordial invitation to the commission to inspect his exhibit at the American Museum. As they entered the crowded building, they were amazed to see a perfect reproduction of the waterfall, with water cascading over the famous brink—but it was only eighteen inches tall! One barrel of water kept it running for a whole week!

This was the day of the dime museum and competition among managers was keen. Constantly in search of new acts, Barnum traveled back and forth across the country, always looking for freaks, natural curiosities, and anything notable. When he heard that Daniel Webster was to deliver an address at the dedication of Bunker Hill monument, he hastened to Charlestown hoping that he could persuade Mr. Webster to repeat the speech in his museum. But he never heard that much-quoted address, for at the foot of Breed's Hill he saw huddled under a tattered canvas tent, something far more exciting than Daniel Webster: a herd of wild, American buffalo!

At least, there were fifteen young buffalo calves which a rancher named C. D. French had rounded up on the western plains and driven across the country. They were so starved their ribs stuck out from their scraggly sides, and when they walked, they wobbled. Barnum bought the herd and shipped them under cover of darkness to his farm in Bridgeport, Connecticut. French went along for thirty dollars a month to take care of the animals.

By restricting their exercise and stuffing them with good feed, Barnum, in two months, had somewhat better-looking buffalo. He sent the fatted calves to a friend in Hoboken, New Jersey. But he hadn't the slightest idea what to do with them until one day he remembered a picture of buffalo being chased by Indians in his grammar school geography. Phineas concocted a report which he sent to a New York paper, describing a recent buffalo hunt staged on the western ranch of Mr. C. D. French. "Fifteen of the most lively and savage beasts were rounded up and will be shipped to New York, from which port they will sail for Liverpool to be exhibited before royalty." He signed a fictitious name.

A few days later "someone" wrote to the editor. "If this herd of wild buffalo are to be in New York, why can't they be shown to the American public? Many of our citizens have never seen a buffalo."

The idea caught on and there was an immediate demand for an exhibition. It was then that Phineas T. Barnum stepped into the picture. He stated he would gladly pay a dollar to see the buffalo and urged that a hunt be staged either in Harlem or on the Long Island race course; or better still, in Hoboken. He himself would furnish Indians and cowboys for the event.

By coincidence, flyers appeared overnight announcing that a buffalo hunt had been arranged for August 31, 1843. Huge billboards blossomed with sensational scenes:

snorting herds of buffalo thundering across the plains pursued by yelling Indians and flying arrows. Bringing up the rear was that noted cowboy, C. D. French, brandishing his rifle. Because this was to be an educational event, the show would not cost a cent; it would be free for all!

"No one needs to be alarmed over the possibility of these ferocious animals charging the multitude," the papers said, "because a stout double railing has been installed all around the field."

August 31 was a hot, fair day, and by ten o'clock in the morning, every ferry to Hoboken was jammed and extra boats were put on. Still the crowds came. They bought bushels of hot dogs and popcorn, and barrels of lemonade, while the New York Military Band played on and on. Barnum, looking around, could scarcely believe his eyes.

Promptly at three o'clock a hush fell over the vast, expectant crowd. Women clutched their children closer, men looked anxiously toward the gate, as a sudden roll of drums and the note of a bugle announced the arrival of the wild beasts from the prairie.

First, C. D. French appeared, dressed up like Buffalo Bill, his long gray hair waving in the wind. Behind him rode several toughies whom Barnum had hired to play the part of cowboys, and following them were the "Injuns," covered with war paint and feathers and yelling continuously. Then, like a group of reluctant dragons, the scraggly herd of buffalo calves stumbled into the enclosure.

They didn't charge; they didn't run; they didn't move. They huddled together, shivering nervously until the vast audience in one mighty roar, booed and catcalled so loudly it scared them and they bolted across the field, knocked down the fence and fell up to their bellies in the mud of a New Jersey swamp.

The great buffalo hunt was all over!

As the sweating, jeering crowd surged toward the ferry boats, they met another mob arriving for the second show. Those who had seen the fiasco couldn't get on the boat and those who had not, couldn't get off. For hours, families milled around the ferry slips in the dark, and it was daylight before the last of the twenty-five thousand exhausted spectators got home. Strangely enough, nobody griped very much because after all the show was free. It cost only twelve cents to ride on the ferry and the kids had had a wonderful time.

Questioned a few months later by a reporter in Boston, Barnum admitted, "It was a rather punk show, but I made over $5,000 that day."

P. T. Barnum had secured all the souvenir, sandwich, soda pop and other concessions, and he had also hired every one of the ferry boats for that day!

What became of the buffalo? Barnum showed them in his museum and rented them to similar shows in Camden, New Jersey, Philadelphia, and Boston. Five were sent to a circus in London and the other ten were put out to graze in the pasture behind Barnum's Bridgeport barn. When their flanks were really filled out, Barnum sold them to the big Fulton market in New York for fifty cents a pound.

All told, those fifteen, flea-bitten buffalo brought P. T. almost $10,000.

II

No Yankee from my home town in Maine ever made a trip to Boston when I was a boy without at least one visit to Austin & Stone's Museum, which opened in 1883 in Scollay Square to do a thriving business until 1913, and to which Barnum frequently contributed acts.

Admission was ten cents and the ticket office was guarded by "Old Jerry," a dummy policeman imported from the London Wax Works, and so lifelike that unsuspecting patrons frequently asked him questions.

Inside was the Grand Curio Hall, a spacious enclosure with elevated platforms protruding from three sides, on which the various freaks and curiosities were exhibited: the living skeleton, the bearded lady, Jo-Jo the dog-faced boy, and so forth. There they sat all day and evening, rising to perform as they were called upon by Professor William S. Hutchings, the master of ceremonies. On the fourth side of the hall were cages for monkeys, a mangy tiger, some tropical birds and occasionally a "denizen of the deep." Spectators stood around, following Professor Hutchings as he strolled from one attraction to the next, describing each act with flowery superlatives.

At the left of Curio Hall was the theater, where vaudeville and skits were put on six times a day. Every time the stentorian-voiced attendant shouted *Stage Show Coming On!* the $3500 mechanical "Vienna Orchestrion" would blare forth an inspiring march and the audience would surge into the theater. You could get a seat in the orchestra for another dime but it cost only a nickel to sit in the circle. It really didn't matter; the place was so small that one seat was as good as another.

While the audience was getting settled, a flashily dressed young man passed up and down the aisle offering the celebrated "Crystallized Lemon Drops—for this performance only, at the price of five cents." The orchestra struck up an overture, the drop curtain bearing paintings of Scollay Square business blocks rolled up, and the master of ceremonies made his dramatic entrance. First, he asked all male patrons to remove their hats and if any refused, a stagehand in a hired policeman's uniform removed it for him. All eyes were riveted on Professor Hutchings—he had thick, black hair, a magnificent handlebar mustache, and on the breast of his cutaway coat glistened enough bejeweled medals and beribboned decorations to make a smaller man round-shouldered. He was said to be both a lawyer and an ordained minister. He had found his niche when, helping a storekeeper add up his accounts, Hutchings discovered he had a phenomenal facility with figures. This led to lecturing at church socials and country fairs. P. T. Barnum, recognizing his unusual talents, immediately grabbed him, gave him the title of "Lightning Calculator," and, not to waste the imposing figure, impressive manner and resonant voice, made him majordomo.

Hutchings came to Austin & Stone's as manager of Chang, the Chinese Giant. He was a fixture there for thirty years, ballyhooing such attractions as Eva Eversole, the Armless Wonder; Hercules, the Steam Man; Niobe, the Vanishing Lady from Paris; and Mlle. Airline, the Human Match.

It was Professor Hutchings' singular privilege to introduce to Boston Barnum's greatest humbug, the Cardiff Giant, which some clever faker had carved and then buried near Cardiff, New York. When "discovered" and exhumed, the apparently petrified remains were proclaimed by Barnum to be those of an ossified giant. This created a worldwide sensation, and no one who heard Professor Hutchings as he eloquently described the colossal fraud, doubted for an instant that he believed the Goliath was genuine. But Dr. Oliver Wendell Holmes visited Austin & Stone's and, when no one was looking, bored a small hole in the giant's head just back of the left ear. Examination of the powdery borings led Harvard scientists to pronounce the Cardiff Giant what he was: the figure of a naked man carved from a block of gypsum.

Hutchings was most ardent when he presented the members of the Fat Ladies' Convention, held in October, 1885. He assured the gaping spectators that additional supports had been installed under the platform to prevent it from collapsing, and with sweeping gestures announced: "Mrs. Hannah Battersby, weight 806 pounds! Miss Ada Briggs, 781 pounds! and Miss Josephine Pollard, a mere girl of twelve, 432 pounds!" As each was introduced, Hutchings would bow, smile, and boom out, "Marvelous! Marvelous!"

Every act was *marvelous* to the professor, and he emphasized his favorite word by jabs on the floor with his heavy, gold-headed cane.

One of the more-or-less permanent exhibits at Austin & Stone's was the "Jumbo Python," an enormous boa constrictor confined in a glass cage. Pointing with his cane, Professor Hutchings would say in deliberate, awesome tones, "Ladies and gentlemen! This terrible man-killing reptile is two hundred years old! He is twenty-three feet long, and weighs two hundred forty-five pounds! . . . Once within his cruel constricting coils, the lion! the tiger! or the elephant! . . . are reduced to pulseless pulp and engulfed into the living vitals of his powerful and elastic body. . . . This is absolutely . . . the largest living serpent ever captured! . . . rival to the giant python destroyed by Romulus! Marvelous! Marvelous!"

Because P. T. Barnum believed that any curiosity would be a much better drawing card if it was "imported from some strange land," he often gave high-sounding foreign titles to his special attractions—The Wild Men of Borneo being an example.

Few of the bug-eyed, open-mouthed Yankees who swarmed into Barnum & Bailey's side-show and then went again to Austin & Stone's to see the Wild Men at close range, ever imagined that those dark-skinned dwarfs who snarled and growled so viciously were, like themselves, native New Englanders.

But that is actually what they were—born, as near as I can find out, in the commonwealth of Massachusetts! According to the few available newspaper accounts, these sad-faced men were the stunted sons of a German farmer who lived on the outskirts of Weston. They never learned to talk or read or write but somehow managed to understand one another. As boys they showed unusual strength, and used to toss each other about when they played in the yard or pasture.

Word of their astonishing strength reached the ears of Hanaford A. Warner of Waltham, Massachusetts, an agent for traveling side-shows. He took them to live in his home and for many years managed their theatrical careers. But it was Phineas T. Barnum who named them "The Wild Men of Borneo." He dressed them in striped suits, braided their uncut hair, and allowed no razor to touch the sparse beards which sprang from their chins.

The banner that hung in front of the American Museum in New York, and later over the entrance of Austin & Stone's, was a masterpiece of scenic art. It depicted in lurid colors the wildest of tropical jungles, filled with creeping and crawling critters, snarling beasts, and slithering snakes. In the foreground, a courageous Yankee sea captain and his crew struggled with a score of hairy, scary savages who, in spite of their diminutive size, defended themselves with wicked-looking war clubs.

Patrons of the museum were thrilled when Professor Hutchings fluently described the little men from Waltham.

"Ladies and gentlemen! These curious freaks of nature are Wano and Plutano . . . the only . . . genuine . . . real, live Wild Men in captivity! They were captured after a terrific struggle, by brave Captain Hammond . . . on the savage island of Borneo. At the risk of his life, and at tremendous expense, he managed to bring them back to civilization. Although they are but three feet tall, these Wild Men of Borneo are as vicious as lions . . . and just as strong! Step up close, folks, and hear them gnash their teeth. . . ." And when these words were uttered the professor would bang his cane on the floor, and Wano and Plutano would rattle the chains that held them fast to the trunk of a stage-prop tree, and emit a few, halfhearted growls.

"Now," said Hutchings, "if some portly gentleman will step to the platform, Plutano and Wano will demonstrate their prodigious strength! You, sir—" and he pointed to a perspiring, two-hundred-pound individual from up country. "Don't be scared, I won't let them bite you!"

Once the big man was on the stage, little Wano, weighing less than fifty pounds, placed his childlike hands on the big man's hips and with a series of grunts, lifted him clear off the floor and set him down some distance away. "Marvelous! Marvelous!" cried Professor Hutchings, motioning for Plutano to get busy with dumbbells, weights and war clubs. The act ended when the two dwarfs grabbed their manager, tall Mr. Warner, and tossed him over their heads.

The Wild Men of Borneo appeared in every large American city, many times, and were also exhibited in Europe. Hanaford Warner made the boast, "My boys are as well known in London, Paris, and Berlin as they are in New York and Boston."

In July, 1949, I gave a radio broadcast concerning the

Wild Men, and over one hundred letters came in, from listeners who had seen them perform at carnivals, the circus, or at Austin & Stone's, and from others who remembered having seen them in Waltham.

Albert E. Chase, of Cumberland Mills, Maine, wrote that when he saw the dwarfs, they were already old men, with thin, silky hair and beards turning gray. "Their hands were as small as a schoolgirl's, but very strong. Instead of being wild, they were almost effeminate."

Mrs. Henry Von Kamecke, who lives in East Boxford, Massachusetts, saw the strange little men sitting on the steps of the Warner boat house, next to the Waltham Canoe Club, watching some workmen as they decorated canoes. "They were very cute in their dark blue striped suits. When we gave them bits of colored string and buttons to play with, they'd smile and stuff the treasures in their tiny pockets."

Mrs. Hanaford Warner took excellent care of Wano and Plutano. She made their clothes and made them long bibs which they wore at meals. They ate more or less like monkeys and banged on the table when they wanted more food. After supper they would sit in their highchairs playing with cards or turning the pages of a discarded wallpaper sample book in which pictures had been pasted.

One day when Dr. Frank E. Whitten called at the Warner home, he found Wano and Plutano wiping and polishing the brass door knobs with woolen rags. Mrs. Warner winked and explained, "I let them shine up to keep them out of mischief."

The door knobs were much lower in the Warner house than is usual. Frank A. Remick of Auburndale wrote me, "They were just a four-octave stretch, or two feet, from the floor; so the dwarfs could reach them." At last accounts, the low knobs were still in place.

Several of the letters I received mentioned that the Wild Men used to stand at the Warners' front window and watch the passing traffic. "Their heads came just to the level of the window sill, and they would grin and wave when children passed by."

When it came time for the Wild Men to leave Waltham and go on the road, Hanaford Warner would cover their heads with black hoods so that folks on the trains and in the streets would not know them. They were covered in the same way when they returned, but ripped off the netting the minute they reached Waltham and raced like happy puppies to the Warner home on Crescent Street.

While attempting to lift a man who weighed nearly five hundred pounds, at Austin & Stone's, Wano lost his balance and fell, the heavy man crashing down on top of him. Wano was laid up for a long time and never returned to the stage. He died in 1905. So his brother Plutano retired, living to be eighty-five—a tiny, wizened, wrinkled dwarf, with scraggly white whiskers and his hair in braids.

I went to the Waltham Public Library and with the assistance of Miss Jane Pride, searched through stacks of old Waltham papers. I found no mention of Wild Men, but in a copy of the *Evening News* for March 17, 1905, was this obituary:

HIRAM W. DAVIS

This death notice was printed yesterday but hardly anyone recognized the name of Hiram W. Davis although he was known to millions all over the world as one of the original Wild Men made famous by P. T. Barnum. His death occurred at the home of his manager Hanaford A. Warner. Mr. Davis was 80 years old and leaves a brother. Both men are less than four feet in height and are noted for their prodigious strength. The remains will be sent to Ohio for burial.

Under date of May 31, 1912, I found this notice:

BARNEY DAVIS

Better known as Plutano, the last of Barnum's original "Wild Men of Borneo," died this morning at the home of Mary Warner, 297 Crescent Street. Plutano was a brother of Wano (Hiram Davis) who died seven years ago on March 16th, 1905. Together they travelled all over the world for more than half a century, under the management of Hanaford A. Warner of Waltham. Upon retirement they came to live in the Warner home. They never spoke English but made guttural sounds and gestures to make their wants known. The place of their birth is not generally known but the remains of Barney Davis were shipped last night by undertaker Orsborne to Mt. Vernon, Ohio.

I wrote to the Mound View Cemetery at Mount Vernon, Ohio, and was told that Barney and Hiram Davis of Waltham, Massachusetts, are buried in graves No. 1 and

No. 2, Lot 52, Section H of that cemetery. Over them stands a simple marble headstone, bearing their names and the dates of birth and death. There is no allusion to Borneo, but across the headstone are these cryptic words: LITTLE MEN.

III

It was shortly before World War I that I came up from Rockland, Maine, to attend the Eastman School of Photography held for one week in Boston's Tremont Temple. Mixed into their talk about lenses, exposures and developing tanks, the boys were gabbing about a vaudeville act that was being presented at the Bowdoin Square Theatre a few doors away, and every day I saw long lines of people waiting to get tickets.

I didn't get to see the show until Saturday afternoon, but the fellow photographer who attended with me had seen it three times. "That Prince Karmi," he boasted, "can float a woman through the air, burn her up alive—and you should see him swallow swords! He's a real Hindu prince from Bombay, India."

We moved at a snail's pace through the crowded lobby and finally were led to seats in the second balcony. I had never been in such a big theater before and it was hard for me to believe that we were going to see all the numbers listed in the program. We watched spellbound the Pathé News; Carlos, King of Jugglers; the Five Bernadettos on Bicycles; the Four Marx Brothers; and at last the main attraction which we had come especially to see: Prince Karmi, the Oriental Man of Mystery.

The theater darkened to the sound of a beating tom-tom and a flute solo in minor key. The curtain crawled upward revealing an oriental garden with splashing fountain, palm trees, minarets, and stars that twinkled against a blue-black sky. We had never had such scenery as that when I was an usher in the Farwell Opera House back home.

As the twenty-five-piece orchestra burst into a fanfare, a noble figure strode into the spotlight. This was Karmi and the crowd burst into tremendous applause. He wore a purple robe with glistening jewels and a high white turban with a sparkling ruby in front, and he raised a diamond-studded sword. Deftly he held up a single blond hair and with an abrupt stroke severed it to show how sharp the sword was.

Two Hindu boys advanced with an upright frame across which they laid swords edge upward to form steps. Karmi kicked off his sandles, and in his bare feet, stepped on the naked blades and climbed to the top and back again without a trace of blood showing.

A young girl came forward and was quickly lashed to a big board. The disdainful Karmi picked up sword after sword and knife after knife, flinging them at the girl—missing her bare arms and legs by fractions of an inch!

Next, a black velvet couch was brought in. On it, in the glare of the spotlight, lay a beautiful woman clad in white tights and a bodice covered with spangles. Karmi, standing over her with outstretched arms, commanded her in a deep, mellow voice, to *rise*. And rise she did, right off the couch until she floated in midair with no visible support. At Karmi's command, she gently floated back to the couch.

Then, while the audience was still clapping and whistling, the Hindu attendants wheeled in a glass coffin. In it, on bright green pillows, lay a girl who appeared to be sleeping. Karmi, picking up a can labeled "gasoline," poured the contents through an opening in the lid of the coffin; then, stepping back, he snapped his fingers. There was a flash of red flames and the coffin was filled with black smoke. When the fire had died down only a handful of ashes remained, which Karmi sifted through his fingers into a vase. With a few magic words and a wave of his wand, he produced a beautiful bouquet of red roses and tossed them one by one to the ladies in the audience.

All of this was thrilling enough but it was the finale that really got me.

A shapely Hindu girl took her seat on a throne and Karmi placed a plaque on her head. On top of that he balanced a small, green, glass ball. A few feet away he placed a pedestal on which was a lighted candle. Putting an ordinary wooden match in the girl's hand, he moved it until the match came in line with the lighted candle and the green glass ball.

Now the stage was darkened; the music stopped; a single spotlight played on Karmi's dark features as he deftly grabbed a rifle and loaded it with powder and ball. Then, removing the barrel from the stock and throwing back his head, he thrust the gun barrel down his throat till only the end of it stuck out between his white and shining teeth. Everybody held his breath. I was on the edge of my seat. Karmi bent low, swaying back and forth, aiming the muzzle of his gun at the lovely Hindu girl on the throne.

The seconds ticked by. And then—bang! Out went the candle; the match in the girl's hand flared up; and with a tinkle of breaking glass, the green ball vanished from her head!

At least, that's the way it appeared from where I sat. Karmi stepped in back of the throne and pried a flattened lead ball out of the scenery and, as the lights came up, presented it to the girl.

That was the kind of vaudeville we had in the good old days!

As the years rolled by and motion pictures took the place of vaudeville, I sometimes thought about Karmi and wondered if he was still swallowing gun barrels and climbing swords with his bare feet. I figured that he probably had returned to India.

I was editing my lecture films in my office one day in 1945 when in walked a short, stocky, man of about seventy who asked, "Are you the Yankee Yarns feller I hear on the radio Friday nights? My name is Joseph Hallworth, and I was interested in your recent broadcast about P. T. Barnum. I used to know P. T. when I was in vaudeville. I played with the Dolly Sisters, and Fred Allen, the Four Cohans and Houdini—"

"Gosh," I said, "Do you remember Prince Karmi? Whatever became of him and those other Hindus?"

Hallworth laughed. "Why do you ask?"

"Karmi was wonderful," I said. "I once saw him swallow a gun barrel. . . ."

"Like this?" And Hallworth picked up my yardstick and, tilting back his head, thrust twenty-four inches of the stick down his throat.

I blinked and stammered, "That's just what Karmi did!"

He withdrew my yardstick from his tonsils, grinned and stuck out his hand. "Shake with old Prince Karmi!"

"You—Prince Karmi? Why, I thought he was a Hindu!"

"So did a million other people. We fooled 'em all, we did, me and the Misses and the kids."

"But," I protested, "Karmi was tall and dark skinned."

"High shoes and brown makeup will change any man. Then, too, that tall turban helped. I even fooled the theater managers. They never dreamed that Karmi was just Joe Hallworth all rigged up."

I was dumfounded. "Who was the woman that floated in air, and you burned up in gasoline?"

"That was Kitty Fisher, my wife. I taught her to swallow things too. And the young Hindus were my sons. That pretty girl on the throne was Willie, my youngest boy. I dressed him in girl's clothes so the act would look bigger. It paid better, too.

"Willie was a princess for ten years, until he had to go to war in 1917. He gave up the skirts and veils then because some of the boys who whistled at him and tried to date him up after the show, belonged to his outfit." By this time I was making notes. "How did you get into this business in the first place, Mr. Hallworth?" I asked.

"I was just sixteen and show-struck. In Austin & Stone's, I saw a man swallow a sword, and it looked so darned easy I thought I'd try it. I went to Wilkinson's hardware store and bought me a flat piece of steel, about three quarters of an inch wide and three feet long. When I got home, I stood in front of the parlor looking-glass and tried to shove it down."

"Didn't it hurt—tickle?"

"Tickle? I damn near severed my tonsils. I gagged and I vomited, but I kept practicing and in a week's time I could shove that iron rod all the way to my belly button."

"And what then?"

"Oh, I knew if I wanted to beat the other guy, I'd have to go him one better, so I looked around for other things to swallow—knives and forks, a Chinese back scratcher and my father's long-handled razor. I knicked my epiglottis a couple of times, but finally got the hang of it. Then I marched in to Austin & Stone's and faced Professor Hutchings. He says, 'What can you do?' and I says, 'Swallow razors, like this—'

" 'No you don't!' says he, jumping up, 'You ain't going to cut your throat in Austin & Stone's without advertising. How much do you want?'

"I figured two dollars a day was pretty good, so he hired me, and for twelve dollars a week, all I had to do was shove everything in sight down my throat."

That's the sort of side show we had in the good old days!

EDGAR WELCH

Only in Massachusetts is April 19 celebrated as "Patriots' Day," and it is always a busy time for the press photographers of Boston. If there isn't a flooded river to photograph or a big Cape Cod forest fire, there is always the re-enactment of Paul Revere's ride to Lexington, and later the Boston Athletic Association's famed marathon race from Hopkinton to Boston, a distance of twenty-six miles.

I have photographed contestants from all over the world winning this classic sporting event but none more gallant than our local veteran Clarence De Mar, who year after year snapped the tape across Exeter Street ahead of his rivals. As I saw De Mar come into focus on the ground glass of my old Graflex, arms outstretched and with a winning smile, I was always struck by his tremendous endurance and by the self-discipline and hard training back of it. And then I thought to myself: Wouldn't Edgar Welch have loved this! He could have won so easily!

Up in his home town of Raymond, Maine, they'll tell

[163]

you, "Edgar was a *born* runner. He'd rather run than eat, and he thought nothing of legging it down to Portland and back in a single afternoon." And that, mind you, is more than forty miles!

Furthermore, Edgar ran in his bare feet and he always went bareheaded too, except for the special trip he made each summer to the summit of New England's highest peak, Mt. Washington. Then—and nobody ever found out why—Edgar wore his grandaddy's tall silk hat.

Whenever the urge came over him to "go higher up," he'd drop whatever he was doing, go home to get the silk topper from his front hall hat tree, jam it down tight over his thick, brown hair, and whistle for his dog, Gyp. Off they'd go, trotting through village and town till they reached the sweet-smelling meadows of New Hampshire that led to shadowy forest glades and the rocky trail beyond, up the steep mountainside.

The sight of this sober-faced, good-looking young farmer, clad in faded blue work shirt and overalls, barefoot but wearing his stovepipe hat, was invariably chronicled in the local press. "Edgar Welch of Raymond ran through town today on his way to Mt. Washington." They knew where he was going because he had on that hat!

Some visitor at Mt. Washington's Summit House, armed with binoculars, was sure to spot Edgar toiling up the trail and shout, "Here *he* comes!" And as if by magic, out from the kitchen would appear the huge tin pail, the lemons and the sugar cookies.

There wasn't much in the way of entertainment on the

mountain in those days, and Edgar was a welcome attraction to guests in the hotel. He talked easily about crops on the McLellan place back in East Raymond and about salmon fishing on Sebago or the plentiful white perch in Panther Pond. And he was sure to describe in detail any unusual bird, or the mother deer and fawn, or the bear he had encountered on the way up. As he sat munching cookies and sipping lemonade, his big, bare feet ensconced in a pair of borrowed pink crocheted slippers, and his tall silk hat still tight on his head, he made a picture hard to imagine on a summer hotel piazza today.

The manager was so pleased to have Edgar run in, he gave him the best the Summit House had to offer, gratis, and urged him to stay till the leaves turned in September. But Edgar never did. He would meander around the rocky, cloud-drenched peak for two or three days, and then as if hearing some mystical voice, he would pause, cock his head to one side, nod, and say firmly, "Well, folks, I gotta go." Without another word, he'd kick off the slippers, get a quick drink of water and disappear around the rocks, his dog beside him. Down the carriage road he'd run, often obscured from view by a passing cloud.

I'll admit this was a funny way to behave, but I don't believe Edgar was as crazy as some writers claim. One old Yankee lumberman summed him up with, "Welch is just a mite touched in his head and rather fixed in his ideas."

When I first heard of Edgar, I drove all over the villages of Casco, Raymond, and Crescent Lake, Maine, trying to find people who had actually known him. Luckily, I found several.

The first was ex-postmaster Clarence Winslow of Crescent Lake, retired and living in a big white house with the most wonderful country kitchen I've ever seen. It was Saturday and the perfume of baking beans and steaming brown bread hung in the clean Maine air. We sat with our notebooks at a big kitchen table while Host Cad Winslow settled comfortably into a rocker where he could look out through the morning-glory blossoms to the village square beyond.

"Sure," he said. "I knew Welch all his life. He used to work for me in the mill. Mighty good hand too; but kinda hard to understand until you got used to him. He sorta had spells when he thought he had to go places, and no power on earth could keep him from going. I've seen him throw down his tools right in the middle of a big job and say, 'I've gotta go,' and then he'd light out like the devil was after him, and he'd run to Portland or up to Portsmouth and once in a while he'd go as far as Boston.

"When he got back, he'd sneak in quiet-like, pick up his tools and begin right where he left off. Funny, wasn't it?"

Mr. Winslow picked up a folded newspaper, swatted a couple of flies with it, and went on: "Funniest thing about Edgar was the way he started his trips. Say he was going to Portland—he'd dash out of the corn shop across the street, come over and touch the corner of my building with his right hand, then lift his head and begin that dog-trot of his. And by gorry, he wouldn't stop till he was well

into Congress Square. But—" and Cad Winslow laid his
hand on my arm, "if anybody or anything attempted to
stop him or blocked his way, that feller would turn around,
run all the way back, touch the building and start again.
Seen him do it dozens of times!"

At Cad's suggestion, we drove over to Casco and called
on Mrs. Grace Gay in her fine, old-fashioned home. It had
nine spotless bedrooms—two of these were occupied, she
told me, and seven were "kept made up in case of company!" That's Maine for you!

"I remember Edgar very well," Mrs. Gay said, creasing
the hem of her apron between her fingers. "He was always
polite, kind to children, and very fond of pets. But it was
a caution the way he larruped around the countryside.

"I saw him trot into Spurr's Corners one time just after
a big load of hay had tipped over, completely blocking the
road. Everybody else went around the hay, but Edgar
scowled, hitched up his pants, jogged back to his starting
point and set out all over again. By that time the hay was
cleaned up, so he kept on going."

We learned that Dr. J. P. Bodge, who lived on Sebago
Lake, took an active interest in Edgar and wrote several
pieces about him for the *Lewiston Journal*. In one article
he tells about the time a man named Jepson bet Edgar
ten dollars he could beat him to Portland with his team of
fast-stepping horses. Edgar wouldn't bet, but his friends
did. He and the team started from Raymond at the same
time and during the first half of the race Edgar was far
behind. But continuing his steady dogtrot which varied

not a whit up hill or down, he finally overtook and passed the Jepson carriage and was nonchalantly wiping his dusty, bare feet in Congress Square when the horses arrived all of a lather. This was easy as pie for Edgar, for when he ran from Crescent Lake and back he covered almost sixty miles; and his trips to Mt. Washington were more than that.

One year a couple of sports promoters appeared in Raymond and convinced Edgar he should go to New York to take part in a long-distance race. They figured Edgar would win it easily and they would make money betting on him. When they handed him his railroad ticket, he was abashed, saying, "I never been on a train. I—always run."

Anyway he went, and the minute his train reached the big city he wanted to see where the race was to be held. His sporting friends, who had other plans for that evening, promised to pick him up at his hotel early the next morning, but somehow Edgar got down to the arena. When he learned that the race was to be held indoors, and over a wooden-plank track, that settled it.

"How do I get to Maine?" he asked. And he started for home on foot.

I saw some other interesting clippings concerning Maine's famous marathoner. One quoted the diary of United States Deputy Marshal Eugene L. Harmon: "November 24, 1899. This day I saw Edgar Welch running through Westbrook in his stocking feet. It was snowing hard."

And it is said that when there wasn't time to go gallivanting in winter—when he was logging, for instance— Welch would take off his heavy woolen socks and lumberman's boots and wade through the deep snow "to cool off," and then he would slide in his bare feet on the glassy, ice-covered surface of Panther Pond.

I don't doubt this, for Cad Winslow told us, "I remember one time Edgar stopped working with the announcement, 'I'm going to Bridgton—be back tonight.' It was a screeching blizzard outside, but he went. The watch-man let him in around midnight, barefooted. He went in the boiler room and soon dozed off with his back up against the big, warm boiler."

Best of all is the story of Edgar's assault on Rattlesnake Mountain which rises above East Raymond and is mirrored in the placid water of Panther Pond. The David McLellan farm, where Edgar worked off and on for years, is located southeast of Rattlesnake. As the sun slid behind its summit, McLellan's place was in deep shadow much earlier than other farms, causing him to remark, "If 'twarnt for that darned mountain top we would have more sunlight and could work longer in the garden."

Edgar got the idea that he could cut off the top of Rattlesnake, and no amount of arguing could make him change his mind. Whenever he could, and each day after his chores were done, he'd pack his shovel, pick, crowbar and jack screw and climb the mountain. At night he added a lantern and sometimes worked the whole night through, chopping trees and digging out boulders to roll down over the cliff. Dr. Bodge wrote in the *Lewiston Journal*, "Some of the boulders weighed nearly a ton, and as they came bouncing down the mountain side they would snap off trees a foot and more in diameter; to the farmers who lived around there, it sounded like an avalanche."

Edgar kept at this one-man job week after week, month after month, and year after year until he had made a noticeable change in the appearance of Rattlesnake Mountain. The stumps, tree trunks, and huge rocks that he dumped in the valley below made such a pile as to cause a state engineer to say, "That mess of Edgar Welch's is approximately four hundred feet long, two hundred-fifty feet wide and on an average fifteen deep. If all this stuff was made into a monument with a thirty-foot base, tapering to a ten-foot top, it would be three thousand feet high!"

The scars on Rattlesnake were plainly visible for many years, but the mountain peak is now grassed over, and underbrush hides the big rock pile. You can still locate its bulk and see a few outcroppings of rock as you drive along the highway between East Raymond and Crescent Lake.

Medical men often commented on Edgar's astounding strength. None of them had ever known another man who could run so easily or so far, or chop and pile up lumber so fast. They knew that Edgar never perspired—not even when he was working hard in the hottest weather—which led one doctor to say, "Some day, the failure of that man's sweat glands will be the cause of his death."

Edgar heard the prediction and commented, "Oh no, I'm gonna die just like Eastman Bean."

Everyone around Raymond and Casco knew how Eastman Bean had fallen onto a hay fork and been killed, and

Edgar was so impressed by this accident that he used to go around singing in a low voice,

> "Oh, Eastman Bean is seldom seen.
> Seldom seen is Eastman Bean."

I hunted up Roscoe Mayberry, who was running a mill in Casco, and asked what he knew of Edgar Welch and his tragic end.

"Poor Edgar," he said, mopping his brow with a blue bandanna. "He was the best man we ever had for chopping wood; he'd stack up ten to fifteen cord in no time. He was always mumbling about dying like Eastman Bean. Finally I says, 'Edgar, if you keep out of haylofts you won't die that way.' But it didn't do no good. He tumbled off a rafter up in McLellan's barn and a pitchfork went right through him. Funny thing—as if he really did have a premonition."

Amen to that! Edgar Welch never won the Patriots' Day marathon, but he's the only man who ever spent twenty years of his life cutting the top off a mountain!

THE PIRATE'S TREASURE

Many have searched for pirate treasure, but few have found anything. George Benner did. Benner was for a long time custodian of the Marine Museum in Boston's old state house, and whenever the conversation turned to pirates he had his own experience to tell the visitors.

As a boy, Benner used to spend summer vacations with his aunt Emeline Benner Lewis and her husband, on their farm in the tiny hamlet of Middlesex, Vermont, just six miles west of Montpelier.

When Mr. Lewis went away, George's Aunt Emeline would invite her sister Patience to come for a visit. Patience was thin as a rail, wore her hair combed back in a pug, had a sharp nose and chin, and smoked a clay pipe. And she told fortunes by reading tea leaves.

One day when he was sixteen, after lunch in the cool, fragrant farm kitchen, George drained his teacup and shoved it across the red-clover tablecloth. "Please, Aunt Patience," he begged, "tell my fortune. What can you see in the tea grounds for me?"

The old lady flipped her glasses down from her forehead, turned the teacup in her thin hand and said briskly, "Why—I see an old sea chest—and a pirate's chart! If you find this map, and follow it, George, you will discover treasure!" She told him other things too, but he wasn't listening.

That night, as he sat in the sitting room with the tiger cat in his lap, George looked at his Aunt Emeline and said, "Tell me again about that old pirate!"

Aunt Em Lewis sniffed. "I thought you'd be asking about him, after what Patience saw in your teacup this noon." She folded her sewing and laid it on the table.

"Well, that was a long time ago. Your uncle had gone to the village after a load of grain and I was all alone. It was getting dark and I had just lighted the lamp in the kitchen when I heard the stagecoach stop. I looked out the window, and that strange man was coming up the path. He had long white hair and some kind of sash tied around his middle. On his shoulder he balanced a small, brass-bound trunk. As he came close, I saw he was wearing earrings, as sailors used to."

"Wasn't you scared, Aunt Em?"

"I most certainly was, but when he knocked at the door, I opened it. He bowed real polite. He said he was looking for a long lost shipmate who had settled somewhere near here. He wanted to stay over night.

"I told him to leave his trunk in the shed, and showed him where he could wash up. I fried some potatoes and warmed up some biscuits, and gave him a piece of apple pie. Later, as he smoked his pipe, he told me about all the foreign ports he'd been to. Then I showed him upstairs to the spare room over the kitchen. I was mighty glad when your uncle drove into the yard."

"What did Uncle say?"

"Oh, he said it was all right to take the man in, seeing as how it looked like a storm.

"Next morning, the old sailor filled up the woodbox, and brought a pail of water from the well. I remember we had flapjacks for breakfast and he smacked his lips over the maple syrup. He offered to pay for the night's lodging and vittles, but I wouldn't take anything. He left his trunk in the back shed, saying he would pick it up when he came back.

"He boarded the morning stage and that is the last we ever saw of him! What he did or where he went, I don't know, but his chest is still up in the attic under the eaves."

Aunt Emeline paused, running the edge of her apron through her fingers. "It's just where he left it. No one's ever opened it, and no one's going to. I expect he'll be calling for it one of these days."

George Benner terribly wanted to look in the trunk but he knew better than to suggest such a move. He did say, "If you open the trunk, you might find the old man's address," but he got no co-operation from Aunt Emeline.

Months and years went by. George visited the farm less often than when he was a boy but he never forgot the old sailor's chest. Around 1901, when George Benner visited the farm with a young relative from Maine named

George Levensaler, he asked his aunt if he could open the trunk. "If the old man is still alive," he urged, "he must be well over one hundred."

Finally Aunt Emeline Lewis said, "Well, you may open it. But I am afraid you will be disappointed."

They tramped up the steep narrow stairs and dragged out the brass-bound trunk which for forty years had been stowed away with a cradle, a spinning wheel and a barrel of old crockery. The lock had to be forced with a screw-driver. As they raised the lid, an odor of musty clothing filled their nostrils. Under a mess of moth-eaten sailor's togs, they found a roughly carved ship model, several bits of scrimshaw, an old quadrant and a copy of Sir Walter Scott's *The Pirate*. There were no bars of gold or silver, not even one old coin for a keepsake.

They put back everything except the book, and as Benner thumbed through it, a folded piece of vellum fell out. On it was a map of a small section of the coast of Maine near the Kennebec River. The lines were quite distinct, and one small bay was marked with a star. At the bottom of the map were these crudely printed words:

"Stand abrest quartsbolder bring top in line with hill N ½ m it lise 12 fathom NE near big trees under stone."

George Levensaler was so excited that he wanted to start for Maine right then to look for the treasure, but Aunt Emeline said, "Nonsense! You will never be able to find anything from that!"

However, the two Georges read the cryptic message over

and over until they knew it by heart, and spent many hours going over coastal survey maps of the Maine coast. In October, they took the Kennebec boat to Bath, Maine.

They hired a small motorboat and, as they were inexperienced in handling such a craft, they spent a couple of days cruising the Kennebec River around Bath.

After purchasing spades, short-handled shovels, two picks and a crowbar, in a burst of optimism they added several canvas bags.

Early one morning, Benner and Levensaler put out from Bath. Cruising very slowly toward Boothbay, they minutely compared the coast line with the old map. Although the contours of several inlets looked promising, the treasure seekers did not find anything resembling a quartz boulder until late that afternoon. Just before sunset, as they were proceeding along the shore, George Benner saw something glistening a short distance ahead of them.

They swung in. About forty yards from the shore was a large outcropping of rock flecked with mica which sparkled in the setting sun. Could this be the "quartz boulder" indicated on the pirate's map?

Although the distant hill appeared to be farther away than the half mile stated in the message, they lined it up. It lay to the north! Walking in that direction, they came upon one large tree and stumps of two others.

It was getting cold, they had no food with them and they did not dare light a fire; so they went back to the boat and turned it toward Boothbay, where they spent the night. The next day at dawn, they returned to search for the stone they were sure they would find. Tramping around in the matted grass, they located a large flat stone and spent the rest of the day digging around it.

Unable to raise the stone before another chilly night settled in, they spent a sleepless night outdoors. Next morning they went back to the job. Putting all their strength on the crowbar, they lifted one edge of the stone and set a small rock under it. By gradually lifting and pushing rocks underneath, they were able at last to get the big flat stone out of the way, revealing a circular splotch of loose brown earth tinged with rusty red.

Levensaler pawed away some of the dirt, saying, "Hand me one of those spades." As he scooped away the soft earth, he uncovered the remains of a wooden cask.

George Benner picked up a hard round object black as your hat. He knocked it against the shovel to shake off the dirt and saw the glint of gold. They had found the pirate's treasure!

More blackened coins were unearthed, many rusted together and covered with greenish mold. "Quick," Benner said. "Get the canvas bags."

Levensaler, reaching into the hole for more coins, brought up something heavy wrapped in a piece of rotting canvas and thrust this into the bag also.

More coins were found as they dug deeper until, at the bottom of the hole, they were so mixed with earth and debris that sifting them out was slow work.

"We'd better get going," said Benner. "Never mind those."

They lugged the bags to the boat and covered them with the tools. Pointing their craft toward Boston, they traveled as fast as they could go. Passing Portsmouth, New Hampshire, in the late afternoon, they reached Gloucester as the day ended.

They got naphtha for the launch and food for themselves, and spent the night on the boat with neither warmth nor sleep.

The following day they skirted the north shore and reached Boston harbor before noon. Without attracting any attention, they pulled in to Northern Avenue pier and tied up. Hiring a hack, they drove direct to the Atlantic National Bank at 10 Post Office Square.

After explaining to dumfounded bank officials that they had found a buried treasure and wanted someone to appraise it, the two men were taken downstairs to the vault and the canvas bags were emptied onto newspapers. It was a sorry-looking mess, but after being wiped with a cloth and brushed, the coins were recognized as seventeenth- and eighteenth-century doubloons, gold moidores and pieces-of-eight.

When Benner came to the sodden mass of rotting canvas and unwound it, he was shocked to find a gold cross nine inches long, studded with rubies and a few small diamonds. Looped around the heavy gold cross was a pearl necklace!

As Benner and Levensaler had no notion of what the cross, pearls and coins were worth, they left the whole treasure with the bank to be disposed of. The gold cross was sold to a prominent Bostonian, and the coins and pearls went to New York collectors. Benner and Levensaler divided $20,000!

Aunt Emeline Lewis, incredulous, refused any part of it. As she said, she had enough to see her through.

My story, "Tea Leaves and Buried Treasure" was printed in the American edition of *The Reader's Digest* in December, 1951, and in all their foreign editions. So I had occasion at that time to recheck the story.

George Benner was living, in very poor health, in the western part of Massachusetts.

The Atlantic National Bank no longer existed, having been absorbed by the First National Bank of Boston, but I found one old Atlantic National Bank employee who remembered the Benner transaction.

The old Lewis farm in Middlesex, Vermont, was no more, having been in the area flooded when the Wrightsville dam was built.

Emeline Benner Lewis died in March, 1935, aged almost one hundred and three. And the old sailor never came after his trunk.

FIRST-HAND GHOSTS

Personally I have never seen nor talked to a ghost, but I know a man who has—Wilfred Robinson of Lynn, Massachusetts.

In 1946, shortly after I told the story of the haunted "Ocean-Born Mary" house up in Henniker, New Hampshire, over station WBZ in Boston, Robinson called me on the telephone.

"You know," he said, "not all ghosts are terrifying, and they don't have to appear in the middle of the night. The one we saw in Hampton, New Hampshire, several years ago, was young and attractive and appeared to us in broad daylight. If you want the details, come over and I'll tell you the whole story."

I made an appointment, and a week later my wife, Alice, and I called on him. Robinson proved to be a sober, serious-minded man. He had just retired from an active career of selling and at long last was enjoying what he had always wanted to do—read. His living room table was piled high with books, mostly biographies and histories. We saw no popular who-dun-its.

He motioned for me to take his easy chair and led my wife to a table where she could use her notebook. He began by saying, "I won't be at all offended if you folks think this story is improbable, but I give you my solemn word it's the gospel truth."

Standing at the window of his apartment, Robinson spoke thoughtfully. "When I was a boy most everyone was interested in spiritualism, and although I was only a little shaver, I was excited and curious. I used to go to old-fashioned séances with my parents. I wasn't scared at these goings-on, just interested and curious."

I knew from personal experience exactly how he felt. In the days before automobiles, movies, and radio had been invented, there wasn't as much to talk about as there is now and what entertainment the country folks had was of their own making. Quiltings and corn huskings and now and then a square dance were common, and out in the sparsely settled communities they had kitchen dances, prayer meetings, and occasionally a séance. I remember dozens of times when my own grandparents held séances in their frigid front parlor, around the big polished table, with the kerosene lamp turned down low. I recall how they would nod and smile or look sad and shake their heads whenever a frosty timber would warm enough to snap, or a board would creak, making what they called "raps." If more than one rap was heard, Aunt Gena would ask in her high-pitched voice, "Is that you, Sister Ellen? Try to rap louder!" Sometimes these spiritualist meetings became lively, especially if the poker-faced young men of the neighborhood squeezed into the circle. Their big, raw-boned hands could always be seen above the top of the table, but none of us could see where their knees were. Sometimes the table moved right across the room, but as soon as the house got warm the raps died down, or the spirits got tired. Then, after a few hymns and thank-yous, the neighbors went home. Grandfather Smith had a big house and if there were mediums present he usually invited them to stay all night; so I had a chance to look them over. I was never impressed.

I judged that Wilfred Robinson had had about the same experience. He turned his gaze from the Lynn traffic and faced me directly, as if up to now he had only been taking my measure. He pulled a chair around facing mine and spoke in an even, dead-earnest voice.

In the spring of 1906, Robinson had had a serious attack of malaria. As soon as he was able, he bundled up and took the train to Hampton, New Hampshire, to visit with his father and mother. Hampton was a clean, quiet country place with lots of fresh air and good food, and at his doctor's suggestion Robinson took a short walk each afternoon, often accompanied by his wife and eight-year-old daughter Edith.

Late one afternoon they had walked along the elm-shaded road which leads from the depot to North Hampton, covering perhaps a mile, when they came to an old red bridge. Here they stood for a short while, looking around, then crossed the highway and started back on the opposite side, along a narrow path. It was the loveliest time of day to be out of doors, warm in the rays of the afternoon sun, yet cool with the breeze from the ocean. The air was sweet with the smell of apple blossoms, lilacs and wood smoke.

Edith, wearing a cape that came almost to her ankles, skipped on ahead, stooping to pick handfuls of golden buttercups which lined the pathway. Suddenly Robinson saw her stop, then slowly back toward him, and he heard her say, "Daddy, that boy . . . I'm afraid. . . ." And as he looked, he saw the figure of a boy standing on the grass in front of an old white house. He was a most unusual lad because he seemed to be brighter than his surroundings. He fairly glowed.

"Well, how was he dressed? How old was he?" I asked.

"Oh, I should say he was about twelve—a very handsome little chap," Robinson answered. "He had a sailor's cap perched on his head, and a big curl of dark brown hair fell across his forehead. His eyes were bright and sparkling and his lips were parted a little in an odd sort of half-smile. He stood with his bare brown feet wide apart and his hands jammed into his overalls pockets. As we walked toward him, I noticed that he hadn't moved or even looked at us; so to call his attention I said, 'Hello, Sonny. Do you live here?'

"The rest of the words died on my lips, because the instant I spoke, that barefoot boy faded into nothing. He didn't jump or run away, he just melted out of sight right in front of our eyes. I will never forget it!"

Robinson went to a desk and brought out some papers. Then he said solemnly, "Blackington, you can't imagine how I felt. I'd heard of such things, but this was the first time I'd actually *seen* one!"

Robinson looked at his notes and continued.

He had been so curious that he went up on the lawn and examined the grass to see if anyone had been standing there, but nothing showed. There did seem to be a cold, damp draft of air where the child had been.

As they walked along, the little girl said, "Where did that boy go to?" And her father answered, "I don't know where he went, or where he came from, Edie, but I'm going to find out." His wife didn't say a word; she was too astounded!

They were so disturbed by what they had seen, they couldn't think of anything else. They were careful not to talk in front of Edith while she was getting ready for bed, but after that, as they sat in front of the fireplace, Robinson kept saying over and over, "Who could that barefoot boy be? And why did he appear to us?"

When he went to let the cat out that night, he saw the glow of a cigar on the veranda next door. Horace Lane, the town clerk, lived there; so Robinson crossed the yard and spoke to him.

"Mr. Lane, I want to ask you something. . . ."

Lane invited him to sit down on the porch, asked about his health, and then waited.

"I want to tell you what happened this afternoon," Robinson began, "and I don't want you to say a word until I finish." Then he told Lane about seeing the barefoot boy, and how he had vanished into thin air.

Horace Lane gasped. "Well, by Godfrey! So he's come back again, eh? So you folks have seen him! Well, by Godfrey!"

"You recognize him? You know who he is?"

"Of course I do. That's Val Marston. As I remember, he was playing with an old gun up in the woods and it exploded . . . nearly blew his hand off. Blood poisoning set in and he died; they buried him down here in the cemetery. Quite a number of folks in town claim they've seen him. I never took any stock in it. Well, by Godfrey!"

Robinson was trembling. "Who else has seen him?"

"I understand the folks who bought the Marston farm have. The Sanborns. You've seen him—short, thick-set man. Goes by here every morning and afternoon. Why don't you ask him?"

A few afternoons later as Robinson walked by the old white house, he saw the owner sharpening a scythe. He stopped, passed the time of day, talked about the weather and the crops, and then asked, "How do you city folks like living out here in the country?"

Sanborn said, "We like it fine . . . now. We didn't at first."

"Ever see anything *strange* around here?" asked Robinson, smiling rather knowing-like.

Sanborn blinked with surprise. "So you know about Val? Well, at first the womenfolks were upset, but we've seen him so often, and he's so pleasant, we think of him now as one of the family."

The farmer mopped his brow with a bandanna and said eagerly, "Let me tell you what happened one day. My wife was coming downstairs with some blankets she was going to hang on the line, and there in the kitchen door stood the boy, with sunshine all around him like a halo, and holding some violets in one hand. She spoke to him, but he just melted away. Since then we haven't seen him, but I'm glad to know he's back."

As Robinson finished telling me his story, he sighed. "I never went back to Hampton, and that's all I know about it. You might look around there some time. . . ."

Skeptical but curious, the next time we drove through Hampton we turned off the main road and went into the Town Hall. William Brown, a tall, rugged chap, nodded pleasantly and listened as I asked for information "about a boy named Val Marston who died of blood poisoning some time prior to 1906."

"Guess I can find that case," he said, reaching for a stack of dusty old date books. In a few minutes he added, "Guess this is what you want: *Valentine Marston, son of C. C. and*

M. A. Marston. Born February 14, 1879. Died October 12, 1890."

Then he suggested, "I've heard he died of blood poisoning, but if you want any details, why don't you get them from his brother—Chester Marston, the barber in that shop around the corner?"

It was almost noon when I went in the barber shop. A tall, thin man was cleaning up and a younger chap was helping him. I said, "Mr. Marston? I want to ask about your brother—the boy who had the accident."

He began to tell me what a remarkable child Val had been, and when he paused, I mentioned casually that a man named Robinson had seen his spirit.

At first, I didn't know what Chester Marston was going to do, but after a tense minute of silence, he jerked his thumb toward the door. "Get in my car. I'm going up to my house for lunch, and we'll talk there."

He didn't say a word on the way, but when we entered his kitchen he spoke to his wife. "Mother, this is a friend of Val's. Will you get his picture?"

She set aside the dish of string beans, wiped her hands, and went upstairs, returning after a while with an old-fashioned picture in a silver frame.

Marston said, "Being born on February 14th, Mother named him Valentine, and if I do say so, he was a handsome fellow, with the sweetest smile. . . . He was plumb crazy over boats and sailors; used to wear a sailor cap, and when he walked or stood he'd sort of straddle, playing that he was bracing himself on a rolling deck."

[187]

Of course the daguerreotype was taken long before Val met with the accident. He was wearing a dress when he sat in front of the camera but there was no mistaking the big brown curl that fell across his forehead!

II

The morning that Mrs. Franklin D. Roosevelt told her radio listeners that she had felt Abraham Lincoln's presence in the White House, I was chasing a two-alarm fire in East Boston; so I didn't hear the broadcast, but a lot of my own radio audience did, including Alvin D. Bulman of Everett, Massachusetts.

He wrote me that he'd had an experience with Lincoln's ghost; so I invited him to come in to Boston and tell me all about it.

He arrived on one of those cold, gray days in February. I was alone in the office, about four in the afternoon, when I heard the elevator stop, down the hall, then the sound of shuffling steps and the tap of a cane coming along the corridor.

Mr. Bulman had on a huge cloth cap, dark glasses and earmuffs, and his frail form was all bundled up in a thick overcoat beneath which I saw the neatly buckled galoshes which kept his feet free of mud and slush. He carried his stout cane in one mittened hand while in the other he held a battered brief case.

"If you're Blackie," he wheezed in a tight, thin voice, "I'm Bulman. Been listening to your Yankee Yarns for years, and I've got a better story about Abe Lincoln's ghost than Eleanor Roosevelt."

He stood his cane in the corner, removed his colored glasses and we shook hands. I motioned him toward the big chair. Before he sat down, he unwound several yards of the thick woolen muffler from around his neck; then I helped him to take off his big coat, but the galoshes he kept on. He was over eighty years old, I learned, and he had braved the biting wind and slippery streets, to say nothing of the crowds in the subway, just to tell me this story. Once out of his heavy coat, he looked so small and thin that a breeze might have blown him away.

Before his retirement, he told me, he had been a reporter on the Boston *Post*, and for nearly twenty-five years he had been attached to the Office of the Attorney General of Massachusetts as a special investigator.

His blue eyes twinkled as he snapped, "I'd know you were from Maine all right, with that Yankee twang. I'm more of a southerner, suh—born in old Virginia."

He told me that his great grandfather, Colonel William Campbell, had been a personal friend of George Washington, and that during the Civil War his father was the only Union white man in the whole county. "My sister," he went on in his thin rasping voice, "helped the Union cause by writing secret messages with a quill pen on cigarette papers, which were then smuggled by northern spies through the enemy lines."

Reaching a thin hand toward his brief case, he brought forth a shining brass belt buckle, and holding it tenderly, the little old man said, "My brother, David Bulman, was conscripted into the Confederate army, but he escaped, made his way to Richmond, and was hidden with some other chaps in the cellar of the famous northern sympathizer, Elizabeth Van Lew."

He blew his nose on a magnificent red bandanna and continued: "She gave my brother David some important dispatches for General Benjamin Butler, and when Dave got through the lines and delivered them at Fortress Monroe, he enlisted at once in the Union army and General Butler was so impressed by the boy's courage he gave him this buckle. There's the general's initials—B.F.B.—for Benjamin F. Butler."

After I had examined the buckle, which has been carefully preserved and polished, I asked about Abraham Lincoln and the White House. Bulman was warmed up by now, but first, he said, he wanted to tell me how he happened to get interested in ghosts.

"I was a cub reporter on the Baltimore *Star* then, and I was sent out by the city editor to investigate the strange sights and sounds going on every night in the old Patterson mansion."

The house had been vacant for years and most folks thought it was haunted. The Bonapartes, who owned the estate, gave young Bulman a key and he slept in the empty mansion for several nights. He found that all the strange noises could be accounted for by natural conditions, and his explanatory article in the Baltimore *Star* caused a lot of comment. With the ghosts explained away, Charles

Bonaparte was able to get a tenant for the house; he sent Bulman a hundred dollars and everybody was happy.

This led to other stories in the *Star* concerning spirit rappings, strange lights and queer noises in "haunted" houses, and finally to a sweeping investigation of the fake mediums and fortunetellers who were doing a land-office business in Baltimore.

Bulman was engaged in exposing these impostors when a total stranger stepped up to him and said, "I would like to take you to a séance some night, over in Washington. I guarantee you'll never forget it." Bulman agreed, and they made a date.

The séance was held in a three-room apartment over a corner saloon, not far from the Pennsylvania Station, and it was conducted by a Mr. and Mrs. Ross. Mr. Ross was over six feet tall; he was completely bald, had a clean-shaven upper lip but wore a small tuft of whiskers on his chin. His wife, the "materializing" medium, was short and stout, weighing at least two hundred-fifty pounds.

Ross offered to show Bulman the cabinet from which the spirit forms would come, and Bulman examined it carefully. It was simply a wooden cage, placed in an alcove between a window and a chimney, with a brown cloth curtain hung in front. The cage was made of light wood, covered with ordinary chicken wire, and had a single door which could be fastened with a padlock. Inside the cage was a large, heavy chair where the medium sat during the séance.

When a dozen or so people had been seated and had

[191]

sung a few hymns, Ross handed Bulman a key. "You take charge of this," he said. Mrs. Ross squeezed through the narrow door of the cage and sat down in the chair. As Ross motioned for Bulman to snap the padlock, the medium leaned forward and whispered, "I want you to promise me that if there should be a fire in this building tonight, you won't leave until this door is unlocked, and I am helped out of here."

Bulman promised, snapped the lock, and dropped the brown cloth curtain. As he went back to his seat in the semicircle of men and women, he noted that the gas lights had been turned low. The séance was about to commence.

After perhaps eight or ten minutes of silence, punctuated by the sound of a few nervous coughs, there came from the alcove the sound of rattling curtain rings. The brown cloth lifted, and out from its shadowy folds appeared the figure of a little girl.

"She didn't walk, Blackie," Bulman told me. "She just glided, right over to my chair, and she said in a child's voice, 'Mr. Bulmer or Bulmay, I am going to tell you something. You are expecting a baby at your house. It will be a boy.' "

The old man pounded the arm of his chair and shouted, "And, she was right! My son was born just three days later. Not a soul in Washington, besides me, knew about that!"

I had to keep reminding Bulman that he had come to talk about the ghost of Abraham Lincoln, and after a while he got around to it, but not until he had told me more about the séance. Besides the spirit of the little girl, there were several other "manifestations"—a soldier who had been killed at the Battle of Bull Run, an old sea captain, and finally there emerged from the shadowy drapes the figure of a tall, dignified woman. She was instantly recognized by a man in the room who leaped to his feet and bowed from the waist. They held a whispered conversation. All of a sudden the others heard him say, "I have risked my life several times in his defense, and you can rest assured I shall risk it again if need be!"

The tall woman seemed much pleased and faded from view.

Other ghostly figures floated out of the cage and then the séance was over. The lights were turned up. Bulman unfastened the padlock and helped Mrs. Ross from her chair. She was pale as a sheet and her hands were clammy. Then he turned to Mr. Ross.

"Do you know the man who talked so earnestly with the woman?"

Ross said, "I'll introduce you— This is John Kenney, personal bodyguard to President Harrison."

That statement Bulman took with a grain of salt, and as the hour was late, he thanked Mr. and Mrs. Ross for a most unusual evening and hurried to catch the midnight train back to Baltimore.

Bright and early the next morning, Bulman was back in Washington, determined to get a story and fully expecting it would end as all the others had. He went first to interview the saloon keeper who owned the building where the séance had been held. "Tell me about those people upstairs," he said. "When they moved in, did they hire any carpenters or cut any trap doors?"

"You just bet they didn't!" said the landlord. "I wouldn't stand for that! But there's nobody there now; go look for yourself."

Bulman spent an hour or more in the rooms on the second floor. He peeked and prodded all around the alcove and carefully examined the walls and floor under the heavy chair. He could find nothing out of the way.

Then Bulman set out for the White House. He walked up to the door and rang the bell and waited. Soon the door opened, and there stood John Kenney. His first words were, "I've been expecting you all this morning."

Just to break the ice, Bulman handed the man his card and asked, "Tell me, how did you get this job of guarding the President?"

"Well," Kenney said, "I was a plainsman out in South Dakota. Mr. Harrison came out with a hunting party and I was engaged to act as guide and cook for them. He saw I was handy with a six-shooter and so later he offered me this job and I moved to Washington."

Bulman asked, "Would you mind telling me who the woman was—the spirit—who spoke to you last night at the séance?"

"No, I don't mind. But you must promise not to print this while I am alive. That woman was the late Mrs. Benjamin Harrison. She died, you know, right here in the White House."

Bulman swallowed hard and inquired, "But why does she appear to you?"

"Why? I guess because I was kind to her. Time and again when she was sick, I carried her in my arms out to the porch and back. Before she passed away she asked that I be one of the pallbearers, and I was."

Bulman looked the President's bodyguard straight in the eye. "Why do you go to these séances, Mr. Kenney?"

He rubbed a big rough hand across his forehead. "I've wanted to tell someone about this for a long time. You see, I'm on duty here daytimes one week, and on nights the next. I had been here about three or four months when I was awakened one night by the sound of measured footfalls crossing this foyer, then going upstairs. My first thought was that somebody was prowling around; then I realized the footsteps weren't light and stealthy but heavy and regular. I grabbed my six-shooter in one hand and dark lantern in the other and went to investigate. I couldn't see a darn thing, but I could still hear footfalls ahead of me. I followed them up the stairs two at a time, and along the corridor, and down the back stairs to the cellar. I never saw a darn thing, but I tell you I was sweating blood!

"A few nights later I heard the same thing about two o'clock in the morning, and I made up my mind that if it was the President himself, I'd give him a calling-down for prowling around in the dead of night and scaring me so.

"That went on for a month, night after night. It got so I couldn't sleep and I couldn't eat. I was worried to death. I never thought it was anything but a human being—I never dreamed of such a thing.

"The President noticed that I was peaked and nervous and said, 'You'd better see my doctor. There is something wrong with you.' But I knew there wasn't anything he could do as long as those footsteps persisted."

Bulman asked impatiently, "Well, what finally happened?"

"A rather strange thing," said John Kenney. "I was walking down Sixth Avenue one day and I met a friend of mine. He remarked on my haggard look, and feeling I had to unburden myself, I told this man what was bothering me. He said, 'Haven't you ever heard the story about Abraham Lincoln's footsteps being heard in the White House?' I said, 'Sure, I have heard that yarn, but I never took any stock in it.' Well, sir, my friend said he knew of a place where materializations took place and suggested we go. 'Maybe,' he said, 'we can clear up this mystery.'

"We had the same kind of séance as last night, in that same room over the saloon. They turned down the lights, we sang hymns, and then those brown curtains parted—and the first figure to emerge was Abraham Lincoln! I had seen him and I knew him. He came straight to where I was sitting, and in that deep voice of his he assured me it was his footsteps I'd been hearing and not to be troubled about them.

"I pleaded with him, 'Mr. Lincoln, please do not do it any more. I am guarding the life of President Harrison now, and you have got me so scared I can't do my duty.'

"Lincoln nodded his shaggy head and smiled. And from that time on, I haven't heard any more footsteps at night in the White House."

THE
KRONPRINZESSIN CECILIE

$\mathbb{B}$OUND for her home port of Bremen via Plymouth, England, and Cherbourg, France, the big North German Lloyd liner *Kronprinzessin Cecilie* eased out of her berth in New York a little after midnight on Tuesday morning, July 28, 1914. Because of thick fog, she made only 196 miles the first day out, but on Wednesday the weather cleared a bit and the *Kronprinzessin* speeded up to 536 miles a day, and maintained that speed on Thursday and Friday, which brought her within two days' sailing time of the English coast.

At eight minutes past ten o'clock on that Friday evening, the wireless operator on the *Kronprinzessin* was receiving a routine commercial message which suddenly broke off in the middle of a sentence. There was a brief pause, then a code signal indicating that an urgent message was coming. The operator adjusted his dials to get better reception, and took down the message:

THE KRONPRINZESSIN CECILIE

BERLIN . . . JULY 31 1914 . . . URGENT AND CONFIDENTIAL
FOR CAPTAIN CHARLES POLACK KRONPRINZESSIN CECILIE
. . . ERCHARD HAS SUFFERED SEVERE ATTACK CATARRH OF
BLADDER (SIGNED) SIEGFRIED

He tore off the sheet, sealed it in an envelope, scribbled "Urgent-confidential for Captain Polack" and sent it at once to the bridge.

Captain Polack read the cryptic message. For a few minutes he was completely puzzled. "Erchard? I don't know anyone by that name!" Then, studying the signature, he remembered!

When he had been commissioned captain of the *Kronprinzessin Cecilie* in 1912, an Imperial German officer had handed him a stout manila envelope. "This packet contains sealed orders," he was told. "Open it only if you receive a wireless that some member of the royal family is ill. It will be signed *Siegfried*." He had put the envelope in a special place in his file.

He went to his cabin to get it. Breaking the seal, he pulled out a smaller envelope carefully wrapped in oiled silk. Withdrawing a single sheet of heavy white paper, he read:

England, France and Russia have declared war on Germany. Take your ship to a neutral port at once.

Unbelievable as it seems, the message had been prepared two full years previously! The only error was that Russia had not declared war on Germany at that time.

With trembling fingers Captain Polack put the paper in his pocket and returned to the bridge.

A few minutes later, strolling along the deck, F. C. Hock, a Chicago businessman, noted with a sense of unbelief that the moon, which had been off the bow, was now dead astern. "That's funny," he thought. "We must have turned around!" And the ship seemed to be traveling faster.

Captain Polack had already silenced the wireless and ordered members of the crew to bring blankets and drape them over the deck lights when, white-faced, he strode onto the ballroom floor and motioned the orchestra to stop playing. In a strained, husky voice, he said, "I would like to have all the gentlemen come to the smoking room!"

When they had crowded around him, Captain Polack said gravely, "I have bad news. War has been declared. I have been ordered by the German government to take this ship to a safe port. We are heading back to America."

The passengers were aghast! Before the chorus of complaints and curses arose, Captain Polack continued, "I want everyone to go to his stateroom. Either darken the porthole or put out the lights! You must not smoke on deck! Even now we are being hunted by British and French destroyers!"

Most of the 1200 passengers accepted the change in plans philosophically, but some of the business men, anxious to get to London or Paris, objected. One group threatened to sue the North German Lloyd line for breach of contract. An exasperated Brooklynite grabbed Captain Polack's arm and shouted excitedly, "I'll buy the ship! Then she'll be a

Yankee boat and no one will dare to disturb her!" But Captain Polack had his orders from Berlin and intended to obey them.

Suddenly all the lights on the decks went out and, in the darkness which followed, the passengers stumbled down dimly lit companionways to their staterooms where they stuffed shirts, sheets, anything they could get hold of, over the portholes to keep their lights from showing.

Those who rushed to the wireless office to send messages to relatives at home felt comforted. But, as Eliot Wadsworth, a passenger from Boston, explained afterward, "We learned next morning our messages never left the operator's desk, and that no wireless messages would be sent from the *Kronprinzessin Cecilie* for fear of giving away our location."

All through the night, along the shadowy decks, sailors scampered with ropes, ladders and paint pails. Bo'sun's chairs were flung over the side and workmen were soon chipping off the bow the big gold letters that spelled *Kronprinzessin Cecilie*. Other crewmen climbed to the tops of the four giant funnels to paint black tips on the stacks to fool the enemy into thinking this German ship was a White Star liner. Like the ghost ship she was, the *Kronprinzessin Cecilie*, through the darkness and gathering fog, plowed toward the far-off shores of the United States "full speed ahead."

Some of the passengers got panicky. "We're going too darn fast in this thick fog," they said. "If we ever hit anything, we'll sink faster than the *Titanic* did!" And so a round-robin petition was prepared and signed by over a hundred passengers. When it was handed to Captain Polack on the bridge, he shook his head. "Sorry, we can't take a chance of being captured. We have a valuable cargo."

He did, however, order the fog horn to be sounded, and every few seconds during the next two days and nights of pea-soup fog and rain, the horn moaned its sullen warning. It was still sounding when the *Kronprinzessin*'s engines slowed down as she approached the coast of Maine.

No one aboard the huge liner had any idea where they were. In fact, the ship's pool had been changed so that the betting was on what port she would put into when she reached the United States. But nobody had guessed Bar Harbor. It was a startled lobsterman, pulling his traps early on that warm morning of August 4, 1914, who informed them that they were safe in the neutral waters of French-man's Bay!

On board was a member of the Eastern Yacht Club of Marblehead. Thoroughly familiar with the harbor, he guided the *Kronprinzessin Cecilie* in close to shore, where she anchored.

Nobody for fifty miles around talked about anything else. The giant ocean liner seemed to fill the whole harbor —a U. S. destroyer anchored near by looked no bigger than a pea pod. To the folks who lived along the coast of Maine, the war had seemed a long way off. But suddenly it had landed in their front yard.

There had been a few significant signs that war was imminent. Both Germany and Austria had large amounts of cash stashed away in the vaults of American banks. Suddenly this hard money had been called home, and about $15,000,000 worth was on board the *Kronprinzessin Cecilie*. Then, too, scores of army and navy officers, scientists, doctors, and professors, visiting the United States, had received calls to return to the Fatherland. One third of the first-class passengers on the *Kronprinzessin* were Germans and Austrians.

The arrival of the German ship in neutral American waters created a delicate international situation. To protect the *Kronprinzessin*, President Woodrow Wilson dispatched two destroyers to stand by. Secretary of the Treasury William Gibbs McAdoo ordered a score of U. S. Customs officers aboard the ship to take charge of the cargo of gold and silver. Mail clerks were organized to sort and forward the 3000 sacks of mail. Doctors by the dozen were rounded up to examine everybody on board before they were allowed to leave the vessel. Coastwise steamboats, including the *J. T. Morse* from my home town of Rockland, stood by to transfer the passengers. Special trains were made ready to carry them to Boston and New York. Every move was covered by reporters, photographers, and newsreel men.

Boston and New York newspapers called everybody they could think of who might get them any information. The Boston *Globe*, to whom I had sold photographs, called me the afternoon of August 4, asking for anything I could get in the way of story and pictures about the German "Gold

Ship." I knew that the *J. T. Morse* would come up from Bar Harbor that night; so I waited on Tillson's wharf to see if any of the *Kronprinzessin*'s passengers were on board.

There were twelve, among them Lieutenant Paul Strauss, an Austrian artillery officer. I had some difficulty understanding his thick, guttural English, but I was able to get from him the story of the *Kronprinzessin Cecilie*'s mad dash to American shores, and also a copy of the ship's log showing her position each day and the weather.

I made a good picture of Lieutenant Strauss and sent it along with my story to the Boston *Globe* that night. This was my first assignment for a big city newspaper.

The American Express Company office at Bar Harbor opened at eight o'clock in the morning, but the cashier, twenty-one-year-old Russell H. Britton, usually arrived there around 6:30. Going to work on the morning of August 4, 1914, he found everyone on the street talking excitedly about the big foreign steamship which had just poked her nose out of the thick fog and dropped anchor.

Wanting to see for themselves, Britton and one of the company drivers hastened down to the wharf where the mystery liner, looming up through the mist, dwarfed the trees and buildings. Borrowing a dory from behind the Eastern Steamship wharf, they quickly rowed out under the stern, where they could make out the name *Kronprinzessin Cecilie*, and her home port, Bremen. A few people were leaning over the rail, some of them lowering strings on the end of which were one or five dollar bills. "Get us a newspaper!" they cried.

Half an hour later Britton, unlocking the Express office, heard the telephone ringing steadily. A Portland newspaper wanted to know all about the big ship. Had her captain come ashore? Was there any truth to the rumor that the *Kronprinzessin* was carrying a cargo of gold and silver? All that day, Britton and the Express agent, Ensor, were kept busy answering similar phone calls.

"I don't recall just how we found out about the money," Russell Britton told me, at his home in Rochester, New Hampshire, in 1949, "but probably it was through the captain. He was trying to contact Olreich & Co., agents for the North German Lloyd line, to get instructions what to do with several million dollars in bullion in the store room. They were within the three-mile limit and it wasn't safe for them to go outside; so they couldn't deliver it in New York.

" 'I said to Mr. Ensor,' " Britton went on, " 'Why don't we go out and talk to the captain? We can ship that gold and silver by express.'

"Ensor was skeptical, but finally we got a boat and went out. An orderly came to the gangway and we handed him our credentials. We were taken on board and escorted to the captain's quarters. They were palatial, furnished with heavy leather chairs, a massive desk, and enormous brass speaking tubes that ran to all parts of the ship.

"Captain Polack was very gracious. He was a great hulk of a man, nearly seven feet tall, with a wind-blown mustache, and his neck was thick as the trunk of a tree. He spoke pretty good English but with a strong accent. He went to a speaking tube and spoke in German, and pretty soon a steward showed up with a tray holding several tall steins of beer. Ensor didn't drink; so I had to drink his and my own. Then the captain said, 'Come below. I want you to see for yourselves.' "

The two Bar Harbor men followed Captain Polack down a long empty corridor to a special elevator which carried them to the very bowels of the ship. Stepping out, they found themselves in front of the vault where two armed guards were on duty. The door was of solid steel six inches thick. After fussing with the combinations, the purser opened it, and the men stood at the entrance of a good-sized strong-room. There was the treasure!

"The gold bars were seven or eight inches long, and three inches wide at the bottom but narrower at the top," Britton told me. "I had expected to see them stacked up, but there was only a single layer on the floor, spaced three or four inches apart to prevent rubbing. A great number of silver bars had been arranged in the same way. Behind the gold and silver bullion, two tiers of stout wooden kegs, which Captain Polack explained were filled with gold coins, stood against the rear wall.

" 'All this,' Captain Polack said, 'weighs over forty tons! Gold and silver are heavy.' "

They went back to the captain's cabin. Their steins had been filled again and a platter of hors d'oeuvres had been put on the table.

"Captain Polack drank his beer like new milk," Britton said, smiling broadly, and continued, "We stayed about an hour and a half talking. Then Captain Polack asked what the cost would be if we shipped the bullion to New York. We promised to figure it and let him know.

"That was my job. The rate would be on the space it took as a commodity, plus a valuation charge. It would come to $7,000 or $8,000, which was more than all the business our office normally would have in a month.

"Of course we did a lot more work on it than that. We had to verify the weight of the gold and silver, decide how to transfer it, and arrange for an armored train to come from New York to pick it up. We did a lot of telephoning back and forth. Finally Olreich & Co. accepted our proposition, and we went ahead."

The bullion was carefully loaded onto canvas slings and, once above the decks of the *Kronprinzessin Cecilie*, was lowered onto the revenue cutter *Androscoggin*, which carried it to the Mt. Desert ferry slip. The wooden kegs, filled to the brim with $4,942,926 worth of coins, were stacked on the wharf like so many barrels of lobsters. The silver bullion was piled up like bricks, then covered with old tarpaulin. The last lot to be transferred was a mere $3,000,000 of coin belonging to the National City Bank of New York. Altogether, the gold and silver were worth about $15,000,-000!

"The first sling-load was taken off the *Kronprinzessin* just as the sun came up," Britton remembered. "But even then reporters and photographers had got wind of what was going on and tried to come alongside in boats, but they were shooed off. By the time we got the bullion onto the pier, there must have been 300 or 400 people trying to get close to the money. But we had guards enough to keep them at a distance."

The special train of steel Pullman cars was waiting, and at Britton's suggestion, long strips of heavy brown building paper were laid in the aisles of the cars. The gold and silver bars were placed on it about a foot apart. The kegs were handled like any freight. In each car, four heavily armed men with carbines guarded the treasure.

They had a green light through to New York with not many stops. At Grand Central station, the $15,000,000 treasure was loaded into trucks like those Brink's uses, and rushed to the Guaranty Trust Company.

The job was over except for one thing: Britton figured that some of the gold might have rubbed off; so he collected all the paper on which it had lain in the cars and had it burned. Eight hundred dollars was reclaimed from the ashes!

The arrival of the *Kronprinzessin Cecilie* at Bar Harbor that summer had an unexpected influence on the career of the cashier of the American Express Company.

Being detained in America, the foreign crew of 800 were unable to get their pay, and had to fall back on what they had in their money belts. So, during the months the ship was in Bar Harbor, the purser used to come ashore every few days with two men carrying ten-quart pails of assorted coins from all over the world. As a service to the crew, Russell H. Britton offered to accept the francs, pounds, marks, and so forth and give in return United States money.

He became so interested in money and foreign exchange, he made himself an expert in this field. This got him into the banking business, and in 1934 he became president of the big Rochester Trust Company, in Rochester, New Hampshire.

After all the passengers and their baggage, and the huge consignment of gold and silver, had been put on their special trains, things quieted down on the *Kronprinzessin Cecilie* riding at anchor at Bar Harbor. Thousands of people flocked to the seaside town to see the big German luxury liner, and I was among them, making dozens of pictures which I still show to my friends.

On November 6, 1914, the *Kronprinzessin* was towed to Boston and anchored with other German ships being held for internment. Just before the United States declared war on Germany in February, 1917, a United States marshal took possession of the "treasure ship" and she was placed in custody of the U.S. Shipping Board. Her crew of German sailors was taken ashore and not allowed to return, but as they surmised that we probably would get in the war, they left the engine room in a shambles.

Nozzles of the high pressure cylinders were broken off, the eccentric rods of the two after engines were reversed, oil lines were connected to the water system, and electrical wiring was rearranged to cause short circuits.

The crew is reported to have cut halfway through the main crankshaft, hoping that some day when confronted by a pack of U-boats, the ship would put on full speed, snap the shaft, and become a sitting duck. Although she was forced to use emergency speed many times thereafter, the shaft held, and it wasn't until after four years of continuous crossing of the Atlantic that the attempted sabotage was discovered.

On July 15, 1917, three months after this country entered the war, the *Kronprinzessin* was turned over to the Navy department and moved from the Cunard pier at East Boston to the Charlestown Navy Yard for overhauling and conversion into a transport by a force of men from the Atlantic Works of East Boston aided by Navy yard mechanics.

There was not a day to lose. The German armies were winning on every battle front, and their submarine warfare was taking a daily toll of American shipping. We had raised a new army of American soldiers; we needed to get them across the Atlantic fast!

To provide sleeping quarters for 4,000 troops and officers, the first-class staterooms were ripped out to make room for standee bunks, extra baths, galleys, and latrines. A whole new ventilating system had to be designed and installed, and the topside fitted to accommodate life rafts and extra boats.

Considerable space was taken by the armament, placed in strategic positions. Six 51-caliber 5-inch rifles were mounted, two on the forecastle, two amidships, and two at the stern. Other guns were set up forward and aft, and all this new installation was connected by an elaborate system of communication.

Given a coat of battleship gray, to which camouflage was added later, the *Kronprinzessin Cecilie* was renamed the U.S.S. *Mount Vernon,* and in company with other German liners which had been interned, converted and renamed, she sailed from Hoboken at 5:30 P.M. on October 31, 1917 with her first load of Yankee soldiers bound for the war zone. This was just the beginning.

After a year's continuous service as a transport, sailing under the American flag, the *Mount Vernon* had her memorable brush with an enemy submarine off the coast of France, on September 5, 1918.

She had discharged her load of troops at Brest and was returning to the United States for another load. On board were 500 passengers, most of them severely wounded soldiers, and several dignitaries including Senator J. Ham Lewis and the blind congressman, Thomas D. Schall, and his wife.

Just before sailing from Brest, Captain Douglas E. Dismukes was handed a radio warning that enemy submarines were operating in ten degrees west and a little north of the forty-eighth parallel. He ordered extra lookouts, as did the captain of the *Agamemnon* in the same convoy.

According to Charles K. Cummings, a Boston architect who served as lieutenant on the *Mount Vernon,* the convoy was proceeding on a zigzag course, the two transports being about one thousand yards apart, escorted by the destroyers

Nicholson, *MacDougal*, and *Wilkes* on the port side of the *Agamemnon*, and the destroyers *Connor*, *Winslow*, and *Wainwright* on the starboard side of the *Mount Vernon*.

The flagship of the destroyer group developed engine trouble and dropped astern, leaving the advanced front unprotected. Suddenly the periscope of a submarine was sighted by the forward lookouts, bearing forty-five degrees and distant about five hundred yards. The *Mount Vernon*'s starboard forecastle gun fired one shot, the projectile landing close to the periscope, which instantly disappeared. Immediately afterward, from the same direction, the feathery wake of a torpedo was seen slashing through the water. It struck the *Mount Vernon* just forward of amidships and exploded with a deafening roar!

From the time the periscope was first sighted till the torpedo slammed into the transport, only seven seconds elapsed, but the whistle had been sounded, bringing all hands to collision quarters; the engines were churning full speed ahead; and a check of the master valve showed that all watertight doors were closed.

The *Agamemnon*, by previous agreement, sheered off to the northwest and disappeared, three of the six destroyers accompanying her. The destroyers *Conner*, *Winslow*, and *Wainwright* circled the *Mount Vernon* and laid down a pattern of depth bombs, which, if they didn't destroy the sub, discouraged any further attack.

The torpedo had torn a jagged hole in the side of the *Mount Vernon* about twenty feet long and twelve feet high, through which more than seven thousand tons of water entered, flooding three compartments and causing the ship to settle ten feet which brought her down to within a foot of her safe limit of buoyancy. But luckily she floated.

Captain Dismukes was on his way to the bridge when he heard the explosion. He immediately sent out a distress call and then gave his attention to steadying the ship. He was gratified that she had only a slight list to starboard and her engines were still turning.

In less than a half hour, the engineer officer reported that the *Mount Vernon*'s speed had dropped to six knots. Two after boiler groups—nine boilers—were out of commission and four after fire-rooms flooded. The engines continued to run, however, because the forward boilers were uninjured. An emergency salt water supply was quickly connected and soon the steam pressure was restored. As a safeguard, the bulkheads forward and aft of the flooded compartments were heavily shored and braced by the ship's carpenter and his men. By ten o'clock, with a speed of fifteen knots, the injured ship turned back toward Brest and reached port under her own power.

In Brest, funeral services were held on the pier for the thirty-six men who had been killed in the engine room by the torpedo. The ship was temporarily patched up with steel and concrete and returned to Boston where she was practically rebuilt for almost 100 feet, a stupendous job accomplished by three shifts of men working day and night.

While she was being repaired, the armistice was signed on November 11, 1918. As she was now called upon to bring 6,000 men at a time home from Europe, extra bunks, four and five tiers high, were built where there had been formerly three and four. On Washington's Birthday, 1919, she made her tenth voyage as a transport. But this time the war was over—her dazzle design of camouflage was covered with a coat of battleship gray, there were no escorting destroyers and lights shone brightly.

On her next voyage, the *Mount Vernon* picked up the vanguard of the returning 26th Division: General Clarence R. Edwards' beloved Yankee Division, the heroes of Chateau Thierry, Belleau Woods and Meuse-Argonne.

As official photographer of the First Naval District, I witnessed the arrival of the *Mount Vernon* on April 4, 1919, from the crow's-nest of the cutter *Ossipee*. But my photographs give no idea of the noise and excitement.

In President Roads, the homecoming ship was greeted by every naval craft in the harbor, by at least a dozen bands, and by roaring, shouting, welcoming crowds on a flotilla of small steamers, launches, ferryboats and tugs, all flag draped, which circled the transport all the way up the harbor until she docked at Commonwealth Pier. For many New England families, this was the real end of the war.

The *Mount Vernon* made one further voyage across the Atlantic and then was berthed at the Federal wharf in East Boston where she remained for four years before being transferred to Solomons, Maryland, along with other German ships which had been converted and had served through the war as good Americans. Eventually they were scrapped.

But the *Mount Vernon* will not be forgotten. Each year,

the men who served on her have met on the fifth of September at some hotel or restaurant to toast their dead comrades and to renew old friendships. When the *Mount Vernon* was dismantled, the government presented a piece of teakwood railing as a souvenir to each member of the "*Mount Vernon* Associates."

Actually, this was the railing of the luxury liner which slid into fogbound Bar Harbor, Maine, in August, 1914, carrying $15,000,000 worth of gold and silver—the *Kronprinzessin Cecilie!*

HOWARD NICHOLS'
BARN

Howard Nichols, pictur-
esque Aroostook County potato farmer, mopped his brow
with a big blue bandanna, but he paid no attention to the
light green worm that was inching its way around the brim
of his sweat-stained felt hat.

"Although I may not look it," he told me, "I'm seventy-
three now. And I can do the work of ten good-for-noth-
ings. Men don't know what work is today.

"I am still plugging away in spite of hard luck." And he
added with a chuckle, "I'm on my third wife and my fourth
barn."

It was not the fourth barn in which I was interested, but
the first. We had gone up to Limestone, Maine, to interview Howard Nichols because he was famous as the man
who had built the biggest barn ever seen in New England.

It was sixty by one hundred and twenty feet, with an ell
forty-four by sixty, and had an attached shed ten feet wide

and seventy-six feet long. It was seven stories high, with metal ceilings, matched wood, seven shades of paint, and over two hundred windows, some of them of stained glass. It cost a fortune. Every cent earned on Nichols' farm for years and years went into it and the thirty-two-room house that had three bathrooms, three fireplaces, a laundry room, milk room, two pantries, an elevator for food and vegetables, and "twelve wash bowls in all."

When Nichols' neighbors on the Caribou road saw that astounding barn going up in 1914, they could hardly believe their eyes. "He's crazy!" they said. "Whoever heard of fancy metal ceilings in a barn?"

"Yeah, but that's nothing! Did you see the four-foot cuspidor in the living room, with running water hitched to it like a dentist has?"

"I hear he's going to charge admission! Nobody around here will be fool enough to pay to see any barn that Howard Nichols builds!"

But they did pay. On some days you could count three hundred Maxwells and Model T's in the Nichols' front yard, and on Sundays as many as a thousand visitors paid twenty-five cents for the privilege of tramping through the barn and outbuildings. It was a great show!

Mrs. Nichols sold pictures and postcards and often took in thirty-five dollars a day. Nichols and the boys acted as guides, and realized an extra hundred dollars a day for their services. On top of all this, they sometimes took in the magnificent sum of four hundred dollars for a Sunday's admissions.

Most of the visitors got hungry, tramping and climbing. When they yelled for food, Howard hopped in his car and went tearing into Caribou. He drew up in a cloud of dust in the depot square, in front of Tom Hartley's lunch room. "Pack up everything you've got, Tom," he said, "and git it out to my barn as fast as you can! There's three hundred folks there now so hungry they're beginning to eat the hay. Here, let me help you lift that cook-stove."

No restaurant ever moved faster than Tom Hartley's. The whole outfit was set up in a corner of Howard Nichols' big barn, and with the help of three short-order men, the air was soon filled with flying hamburgers and apple pie.

P. T. Barnum himself was never as proud of a new elephant as Nichols was of his barn. Only one thing bothered him: it had no weather vane. He sent for one but it looked like a toy on top of the ridgepole. He ordered a copper cow eight feet high and six feet long, and to hold it he had a cupola built, big as an ordinary camp, fourteen feet wide and twenty feet long.

When the copper cow arrived, the whole neighborhood turned out to see her "histed" to the top of the barn. It took twenty men all day to get her up there and balanced properly on the steel spindle which rose several feet above the cupola roof.

As soon as she was set, with her horns pointing west, Nichols jumped in his Ford and drove toward Caribou. When he had gone about five miles, he pulled to the top of a hill and looked back.

"Shucks!" he said. "Can't see it any better than the first one!"

He had already paid more than a thousand dollars but he summoned a firm in Albany, New York, that was noted for decorating state house domes. "Come up here as fast as you can and bring lots of gold leaf."

When the crew of gold-leaf experts arrived in Aroostook, they half expected to find themselves the victims of a practical joke, but instead they found a wiry, bright-eyed little man in working clothes who knew what he wanted.

"Oh," he said, "you finally got here. Well, there's my cow up on the roof. Give her a good thick coat of gold leaf and, if you have to, give her two coats. I want her to *shine!*"

When he saw the cow glittering in the clear Aroostook sunshine, Nichols got in his car, drove the five miles, pulled up on the hill and looked back.

"Thar," he said with satisfaction, "that's something like it!"

But when he got to thinking about that golden cow, way up on top of the barn all alone, he thought, "One vane ain't enough for a barn that size." So he ordered a horse, a trifle smaller than the cow, made up for the ell and for a while they swung in unison with every breeze that blew.

Howard Nichols enjoyed all the fame the big barn brought him but it was followed by tragedy.

One windy day in March, 1924, when the barn had been completed about three years, Mrs. Nichols looked out the window of her modern kitchen and saw a wisp of smoke curling around the barn door. All the farm hands were down in the field—a field that was acres big—and by the time they got there, the barn was a roaring, seething, crackling mass of flames.

Great tongues of fire licked up the sides of the haylofts and with the sound of cannon the heavy steel beams collapsed and crashed upon the livestock. Twenty-two head of cattle, twenty-six sheep, three horses and all the farm machinery were destroyed in a few minutes.

Great clouds of yellow smoke rose over Limestone ridge and drifted for miles. It was the biggest fire ever seen in that part of Maine.

Howard Nichols stood spellbound, watching his life's savings go up in smoke. He saw the swirling sheets of flame lick up to the cupola, saw it fairly explode in the terrific heat, saw angry red flames turn to green as the fire reached the copper weather vane. For just a moment, the golden cow shuddered, then dissolved in a stream of molten metal that cascaded down through the twisted timbers.

A sudden shift of wind, and the fire fanned toward the house. The shingles caught, paint peeled off, windows cracked, and the new house burned flat with practically everything in it, including the beautiful brass cuspidor equipped with running water. Loss ninety thousand dollars. Insurance five thousand.

As soon as the ruins had cooled, Nichols pulled the charred timbers to one side, raked the basement floor, dusted the ashes off the few pieces of salvaged furniture, and with his family moved into the cellar of the barn. It

was cold and uncomfortable but they made the best of it.
They had managed to save the potato house and the granary, and that was something to be thankful for.

But thirteen days later the granary was set on fire and
destroyed and an attempt made to burn the potato house.
Nichols had a right to be discouraged—he had lost everything except the fields which had brought him prosperity
in the first place. So back he went to the rich brown soil,
determined to recoup his fortune. He would start by building a barn.

For seven long, lean years, the family lived in the cellar,
in cramped, miserable quarters. Times were hard and potato prices much lower than when Nichols had made his
fortune. There was new stock and machinery to buy,
never-ending work to be done in the fields. From dawn
till dark, Howard Nichols slaved, racing from one task to
another. For relaxation he would work on the new barn,
not quite as big and nowhere as elaborate as the first one,
but worth seeing just the same.

Then tragedy struck again. His second barn, eleven head
of cattle, and seventeen horses were destroyed in a forty-
seven thousand dollar fire.

Again he built. But several years later, his half-finished
barn, and his house, were leveled by a fire of suspicious
origin.

While the red-hot embers were still swirling about Nichols as he herded his sheep to safety, a sympathetic neighbor
said, "Take that house of mine down the road. Stay there

as long as you want to." So they had decent shelter while they made plans for the future.

"Wonder what Old Man Nichols will do now?" the villagers asked. "If he had sense, he'd sell out and move some place else. That farm is jinxed. He'll never come back now, he's too old."

He wasn't, though. He got up a little earlier, worked a little faster, stayed at it a little longer, and while the house I visited in 1941 wasn't much to look at compared to the thirty-two room residence that had had three baths and a laundry chute, it was a neat, comfortable home.

Long before we reached the Nichols farm, we could see the new, fourth barn and the scaffolding around it silhouetted against the summer sky.

A gray-haired woman and two tortoise-shell cats greeted us as we drove in the yard. The woman was the third Mrs. Nichols, and the cats were "Cheese" and "Crackers."

"You will find my husband down in the back field," she said pleasantly. "You can drive all the way."

We went around the barn, up a sloping hill and saw, far in the distance, a group of workers. As we approached, we saw that one was a girl—a very pretty girl—in overalls. A small, somewhat bent, man came toward us with outstretched hand.

"Name's Nichols," he said, grinning. "And this is my daughter Christina. She's as good as any hired man I ever had." With a wave of his battered brown hat, he shooed her back to work. "Doesn't like to work around the house, though. So last week I says to my wife, 'Let's put her out with the hired men.' She used to eat hearty and groan all night. Now she works outdoors all day, eats bigger meals, and we don't hear a thing from her all night. Sleeps like a log."

Looking out over the rolling fields that extended to the horizon, I said, "I've seen a lot of fine farms, Mr. Nichols, but never a better one than this. How much of all this land is yours?"

He swung his arm in a wide circle. "Far's you can see— all my property. Three hundred sixty-five acres of the best potato land in Northern Maine. Good rich dirt—no rocks, no swamp, no swale. Got nine good wells and a brook on this place. Don't allow no weeds, mustard, or kale here. Keeps a feller pretty busy, though, looking after everything. I got one hundred twenty-five acres of potatoes this year. Hope I can get a decent price. I'll be sunk if I don't. Feller offered me $120,000 for this place once. I told him O.K. but when he come with the papers, I backed out. Just couldn't let go of it—you know how 'tis."

He leaned close to the open window of our car, but refused to sit down. "Gotta keep my eye on the crew," he said. "What else can I tell you?"

"Something about your early life in New Brunswick."

"I warn't more'n eight or nine when I used to help my father and brothers with loggin'. When I was fourteen, I used to haul logs in the day time and potatoes nights. Hauled 'em across the border on a two-horse sled. Had to put the spuds in sacks, a barrel to a bag, and twelve barrels to a load."

He shivered as he recalled those winter nights when the roads were buried under six-foot snow drifts and the temperature was often down to forty degrees below zero.

"I didn't have no overcoat and I used to get an awful sweat loadin', then I'd drive five miles most frozen to death, put the 'taters in the man's cellar, get another sweat unloadin' 'em, and then strike for home and freeze all the way. So you see, on account of making two trips a night, I got four sweats and four freezings. When the last load was down cellar, I'd start for home so darn tired I'd drop right down on the floor of the sled, and first thing I'd know we'd be right at the barn door." His face softened. "Mother would always be waiting for me with a lantern. She stayed up when I was out hauling spuds. She'd come out and wake me and help me bed down the team.

" 'Bout the time I was seventeen, Father wore right out from hard work, and I had to take over the farm. Didn't have no tractors in them days—work all done by hand and horses. Don't see how we ever accomplished as much as we did."

I asked, "Did you always work so hard?"

"After Father wore out I had to. In the winter when it was dark from four in the afternoon till seven the next morning, I used to get some sleep. But in summer, by golly, I didn't get any rest at all, so it seemed." He stroked the two-day stubble on his chin and went on. "Summer's short up here. You have to make every minute count.

"Found I didn't have time to ondress, so for three years I laid on an old couch in the kitchen and didn't ondress only when Mother made me take my clothes off, so she could wash 'em.

"We had to use two teams. Jest as soon as I could see a trace of daylight through the winder, I'd go out to the barn, feed the stock, harness the first team, and go right to work, stars all shining. Come back around six o'clock and grab breakfast. Mother would have the other team hitched up, and I'd start out again. Work till four in the afternoon, come back and set down to lunch, put my hat on the floor 'side my chair, eat, and change horses and work till dark. Folks all to bed when I went out; folks all to bed when I got back.

"That's the way I've worked all my life. And now on account of mean people and jealousy, and three bad fires, I'm getting behind."

He had spoken without stopping to take a breath. Now he mopped his head again and calmly surveyed us. "Come and see the barn I am working on now. It's a pup compared to the big one, but you can get an idea what it looked like."

He stooped over and picked up a rock, no bigger than a walnut; then he found another, and these he carefully tossed on a big pile at the side of the barn.

"My grandfather taught me that trick," he said. "Never go by a stone in the field. Pick it up and put it where it belongs. See that pile of rocks? I been thirty years piling them up!"

He pointed to a driveway that went in under the barn. Jutting from a pile of rubble, blackened timbers, and rusted machinery, the subterranean passageway looked as big as the entrance to the East Boston tunnel. It was big enough for two trucks or three wagons to move abreast, and the opening was nine feet high. Nichols explained that he had tunneled under the hill for 150 feet to permit the roadway to run right into the barn cellar, which had been blasted out of thirteen feet of solid ledge. In the old days, that driveway had run 120 feet under the main barn and the same distance under the ell. The cement walls on either side had supported 108 steel beams reinforced with concrete.

"We used a lot of cement," Nichols said proudly. "There is 400 pounds to a barrel, and we put 1900 barrels into those foundations." He shook his head as he called our attention to the rusted girders and steel beams and cracked cement walls.

"Before I built my first big barn," Nichols said, "I made a six-foot model, everything complete. I had to whittle the pieces with my jackknife and set 'em with glue."

And the contractors had no difficulty in following the model and plans of this illiterate man!

The double hip roof necessitated two sets of purline posts, twenty-four to thirty-three feet long. The roof was sixty-three feet from the main floor and seventy-five feet from the cellar to the peak.

"I had a great system for storing hay and grain," said Nichols. "Kept it in big bins. I built six of them bins and they was twenty feet square. Each bin had two doors, ten foot wide. Them doors weighed half a ton each and we histed 'em with a double and triple block. When they was shut down tight a hen louse couldn't get between 'em. And when they was histed up, the whole barn was open. Folks around here never seen anything like that before.

"I had the prettiest cow barn in the United States," he continued, "with a long cement drinking trough fixed so the cows could turn on the water themselves."

He leaned toward me and almost whispered, "And I had the coziest room fixed up right opposite them, with big leather chairs, table, books, and magazines, and a comfortable couch where you could lay down and watch the cows all night if you wanted to.

"The stable was even prettier," he went on. "Had the same kind of fancy metal ceilings that the best restaurants in New York had. The whole ceiling was covered with big squares painted in different colors, and I put on two coats. Cost a lot of money, but I didn't care then."

The whole seven-story structure was given two coats of paint also, harmonizing shades of gray. And when everything was complete, the great glistening weather vane, the bigger-than-life-size cow, revolved on its spindle eight feet above the cupola.

We went into the new, fourth, unfinished barn and saw at one side the remains of heavy concrete construction. "Ah," said Nichols, "that was what got 'em! That was my smoke house, built right into the cement walls with a special chimney to carry all the smoke outdoors. When we cured our hams not a wisp of smoke could be seen or smelt here in the barn.

"And my granary, eighteen by forty feet, was five stories

high! Look up there," he said, pointing. "You can see where the top of it rested against the wall."

High above us a shaft of rich color began to take shape. First rose, then purple, and finally the deepest blue blended in the haze far above our heads. The afternoon sun had touched one of the few stained glass windows that had been saved from the great fire. The slanting beams of brightly colored light cut through the dust like a search-light.

"I wish you could have seen it before the fire," Nichols said sadly. "It was just like a cathedral, with all them colored windows shining."

"How many?" I queried.

"More'n two hundred. But not all was colored glass. Makes me sick when I think what I paid for stained glass, copper shingles, and waterspouts. 'Bout thirty-six cents a pound for copper, and I had tons of it."

I said, "That barn must have covered quite an area!"

"She had 10,600 feet of floor space! She was a whopper!"

"Nice place for a country dance," I ventured.

"No dances!" he said quickly. "But we did have church services before we put the hay in."

"Church services? What did the people sit on?"

"Pews, of course. Took 'em right out of the different churches round about. They brought the organ, too. Made me feel good to hear them fine old hymns ringing from the rafters of my barn!"

"How did you take care of so many people?"

"Oh, we fixed up rest rooms, and I opened a store down in one corner of the basement so they could buy things, and Tom Hartley had his lunch counter going day and night.

"Some excitement in them days!"

A short time before the Limestone Airbase was started four miles north of Howard Nichols' farm on the Caribou Road, the old man sold his property. His last farm, on Conant Road, Fort Fairfield, was never a success. Buildings which had been old and shabby when he moved there grew even shabbier because he refused to pay more than a dollar and a half a day for labor.

When he died, in 1953, Nichols was chiefly known as a stubborn, cantankerous character. But old-timers still referred to him as the man who, forty years before, had built the big barn.

LAFAYETTE MULLIGAN

Iɴ Oᴄᴛᴏʙᴇʀ of 1924, Edward Albert Christian George Andrew Patrick David Windsor, then the Prince of Wales and heir to the throne of England, visited New England. His stay was strictly a social affair, and weeks before his arrival the newspapers told of his crowded schedule and social engagements, and all the ladies followed closely every word of the published descriptions of dinner-dances, and parties arranged in honor of the prince by the Appletons, the Lawrences and Tuckermans.

His Royal Highness was expected to stay on the North Shore for several days; actually he remained in Massachusetts less than twenty-four hectic hours. After he had spent some time at his hunting lodge in Canada, his special train came down from Montreal, arriving at Lowell on the morning of October twenty-third. Accompanied by several military aides and his secretary, Captain Lascelles, the prince was greeted by his host, Mr. Bayard Tuckerman, Jr., socialite and sportsman, of Savin Hill Farms, Hamilton, one hundred newspapermen and several thousand excited spectators.

Through the gorgeously autumn-tinted countryside, the prince rode to Hamilton, changed, had lunch and then took part in a drag hunt at the Myopia Country Club. He posed for photographers of course, and it's a pity that Kodachrome hadn't been invented, for he wore a chocolate-colored coat, canary-colored waistcoat, bright yellow breeches, black bowler hat and a bright brick-red cravat.

After the hunt, he made a few calls and then motored to Gravelly Brook Farm in Topsfield, where he was royally entertained by the John S. Lawrences. He dined, drank and danced till dawn. Then, not having been to bed at all, he boarded his special train, was whisked to New York, and on Saturday, October twenty-fifth, sailed for Southampton.

A big pile of mail had accumulated for the prince at Hamilton, and the royal secretary opened one registered letter and package which pleased and puzzled both the prince and himself. The missive, on official City Hall stationery, was dated Boston, September 18, 1924.

"Captain the Honorable J. F. Lascelles, Secretary to His Royal Highness the Prince of Wales, care of Bayard Tuckerman, Jr., Savin Hill Farms, Hamilton, Massachusetts.

"SIR: I am directed by His Honor, James Michael Curley, Mayor of Boston, to transmit through you to His Royal Highness the Prince of Wales, this key to the city.

"It symbolizes to some degree the deep regard and respect that the citizens of new Boston have for the mother country and for its prospective sovereign.

"Although His Honor realizes that the prince's stay in New England is extremely limited, he instructs me to say that both he and the citizens of Boston would feel greatly honored if His Royal Highness should find it possible to call, even though briefly, either at City Hall or at the mayor's residence."

The letter was signed, "Your Obedient Servant, Lafayette Mulligan, Social Secretary to His Honor Mayor James M. Curley."

The package that accompanied the letter contained a morocco case in which reposed on purple plush, one of the big gold keys that Curley gave out to distinguished visitors.

If the Prince of Wales was surprised to receive a key to the city of Boston and a cordial invitation to call at Mr. Curley's shamrock-shuttered home, it was nothing to the shock Mayor Curley got when he received a "Thank you" note from Buckingham Palace for a gift which he had not sent and a letter he knew nothing about. And as for this social secretary, Lafayette Mulligan, James Michael had never heard of him!

His own regular official secretary was Standish Wilcox, who was so upset over this prank, or joke or whatever it was, he became ill; he feared that folks would think "Genial Jim, the poor people's friend" was trying to be a social climber, and that would cost them votes.

Baffled and embarrassed, Mr. Curley and Wilcox decided not to say anything about this exchange of courtesies be-

tween Boston and Buckingham Palace, and for two long
months only vague whispers echoed around the corridors
of City Hall. But on December eighteenth, somebody
tipped off the press, and a wild-eyed gang of reporters
pounced on Mayor Curley.

"Where's the letter from the prince?"

"Why didn't you tell us you'd invited him to Boston?"

"And who is Lafayette Mulligan?"

Now, Jim enjoyed a joke as well as any Irishman, but
he had to admit that this one was over his head. He hadn't
the faintest idea who Lafayette Mulligan was, and he most
certainly had not sent the key to the city of Boston to the
future king of England. Not only had Curley been hoaxed,
but so had the prince, and as newspapers all over the world
commented on the case, private detectives were put to
work in Boston, and over in England Scotland Yard investigated. They uncovered nothing.

Most Bostonians believed there never was a real Lafayette Mulligan, until on December twenty-fourth Bayard
Tuckerman showed reporters a letter he had just received,
a letter on expensive bond stationery of a delicate green
shade, with the name "Lafayette Mulligan" embossed in
darker green.

"Dear Mr. Tuckerman: I feel that your silence following
the Mayor's repudiation of his generous impulse in sending
a key to the Prince of Wales entitles you to the last key to
the City of Boston, and I am sending it herewith. Your
Obedient Servant, Lafayette Mulligan, Former Social Secretary to His Honor James M. Curley."

The address on this super-duper sheet of social note paper was 42 Beacon Street, and when reporters tumbled out of their taxicabs there, they found themselves in front of the exclusive Somerset Club. The superintendent, Mr. John Griffin, was visibly shaken when asked if Lafayette Mulligan was staying there.

"MULLIGAN?" he gasped. "A MULLIGAN in the Somerset Club? You must be joking, gentlemen."

The press boys persisted, and Mr. Griffin finally broke down and admitted that many years ago a man named Mulligan had worked there as a handy man, but of course there was no member by that name. Now the beanpot really began to sizzle. Every day every newspaper had something about Lafayette Mulligan. One editorial demanded he be brought before the bar of justice and sentenced to a lifetime of hard labor making keys out of Quincy granite.

The Boston *Sunday Herald* carried a full-page feature with the Mulligan coat of arms, and a long list of distinguished Irishmen of that name. There was Col. James A. Mulligan who died gloriously for the flag in the Civil War; Reverend James Mulligan of Sandwich on Cape Cod; and William Mulligan who was knighted by the Pope for his work among the soldiers in World War I.

In the sporting field, there was "Eddie" Mulligan, shortstop of the Chicago Cubs; and Dan Mulligan of the West Point football team. In science, art, letters, music, the Mulligans had made proud records, and all this caused another member of the noble clan, Mr. Shamus Mulligan, to take his pen in hand and denounce all who would cast aspersions on the fair name of his family.

Said Shamus, "If the Somerset Club wants to mend the damage they've done, they should immediately elect me to membership."

Boston was now in an uproar. Who was Shamus Mulligan? Well, from his photograph, which appeared in every paper, he looked like a cockeyed character from a Mack Sennett Comedy. He wore a square-topped derby, handlebar mustache, wing collar and ascot tie. And he gave his address as Four Bulfinch Street, Boston—the old Argonne Hotel, then operated by the Salvation Army.

"Is there a Mr. Shamus Mulligan registered here?" asked reporters.

"There is," replied the clerk, "but he's not in at the present moment."

A Boston *Globe* reporter handed Shamus' photograph to the clerk. "Does this look like the man who's staying here?"

" 'Tis the spittin' image of him."

So the boys waited and waited, hung around all night, but Shamus did not show up. Like Lafayette Mulligan, he had vanished into the great unknown, which helped to deepen the mystery, and every day new rumors cropped up to keep the story on the front page.

At the dog show, an Irish terrier named "Lafayette Mulligan" won first prize. Babies were said to be named for him, and in the Boston City Council, Mr. Daniel W. Lane— graduate of Harvard and resident of the Back Bay—arose and proposed that famous Lafayette Mall be renamed Lafayette Mulligan Mall. But the motion was defeated.

On February 18, 1925, six months to the day from the time the famous letter was written to the Prince of Wales, the Boston *American* broke the story. In a series of exclusive articles which ran for three days, the late Bert Ford announced to the waiting world that Lafayette Mulligan was in reality Frederick Russell Brine, a reporter on the staff of the Boston *Herald*. It was also disclosed that Mr. Brine's co-conspirators were Albert Gordon (*Herald*) who thought up the name, and Stuart Griscom (*Herald*) who handled the correspondence. Walter Kane (Boston *Telegram*) carried the letters and package to the post office; he had to make five trips before he found a registry clerk who didn't know him.

The photograph of Shamus was an oldtime portrait of a pickpocket, from the rogues' gallery of a near-by city. Copies had been made by Jimmie Jones, staff photographer of the *Herald*, and distributed by the pranksters to all newspapers.

The secret had been well kept. Only four men at the *Herald* knew anything about the hoax, and only two employees of the company where the die and stationery were obtained. This item was their biggest expense—the two-toned, die-stamped fancy green stationery cost seventeen dollars. Postage was twenty-three cents, and the room at the Argonne Hotel, two nights, for the fictitious Shamus Mulligan, was three dollars. Total: $20.23—a bargain!

Mr. Fred Brine himself told me how the famous prank

came about. "Be sure, Blackie," he said, "make it plain there was nothing political intended. I just thought it would be fun to have a fictitious social secretary send that key to the prince. We didn't look for all that commotion on two continents!"

There have been many other hoaxes, of course, but for my money, this was the cleverest and most expertly engineered gag ever perpetrated in the New England states.

MIRACLE
AT ROCKY GORGE

A FEW days before gasoline rationing went into effect in the summer of 1942, almost everybody in New England planned to take a last drive before the use of gas was curtailed.

Up in Glen, New Hampshire, Ade Nitschelm, proprietor of Glenwood Inn, told his guests he would take them to Rocky Gorge for a cook-out and a swim. About eighteen young people piled into two big cars and the hotel beach wagon, among them Dorothy Sparks of Philadelphia, an all-round, out-of-door girl who could ride expertly, ski, and, of course, swim like a fish.

The picnickers set out for Rocky Gorge via Intervale and North Conway. They rattled through an old covered bridge and followed the banks of Swift River. Halfway between Conway and Passaconaway is the gorge, a narrow, rocky chasm with two photogenic waterfalls and a fine old rustic bridge.

The Swift River, which cuts through Rocky Gorge, runs with great intensity during the spring freshets. In the summer it is much reduced except where it narrows above the falls which drop twelve feet into a deep pool. Below this pool, the stream drops again into a second pool, then twists and turns between its rocky banks to the valley beyond.

At Rocky Gorge, on July 20, 1942, the Glenwood group ate a hearty lunch of broiled steak and baked potatoes, topped off with watermelon which had been chilled in a shaded pool. The sun was warm and the pine needles smelled good. It was grand to be young and alive in that wild ravine!

After lunch, they scattered, some going across the bridge and up the mountain trail while others waded in the shallow basins and pot holes, or dived in the pools.

At about five o'clock, Ade sounded his automobile horn as a signal that it was time to start back. There was confusion as everybody scampered around picking up shoes, stockings, and sweaters. Ade counted noses. There were only seventeen.

He asked casually, "Anybody seen Dottie Sparks? She seems to be missing."

"She was on the other side a minute ago," someone said, "over there by the big rock. She can't have gone very far."

Ade went to the bank of the river, looked up and down and called. Then they all shouted, but there was no answer. "Funny," Ade said, "where she could have gone so quick."

Then it dawned on him that the only place she could be was in the river. Probably she had been swept over the falls and would bob up at any moment in the pool below. He waited and watched, but Dorothy Sparks did not appear—and for a good reason!

Instead of crossing Swift River by the foot bridge, she had jumped barefooted from one wet rock to another. Suddenly she slipped and fell, landing on her back with her feet pointed upstream, in the only rapid water above the falls. Unable to catch hold of anything, she was carried along swiftly to the brink. Realizing that once in the deep pool below, she could easily swim ashore, she held her breath for the plunge.

In a matter of seconds, her left foot caught between two rocks and she fetched up on a projecting ledge partway down, her body bent backward from the waist, her arms and head dangling downward and water crashing all over her. She tried to shove her hands up through the falls but the current was too powerful.

In that terrifying moment, Dorothy remembered what her grandfather, a Norwegian doctor, had once told her. "If you are ever caught under water and want to end it all quickly, take a deep breath."

She held her breath as long as she could, then in one last desperate effort, she took a deep one! Instead of getting her mouth and lungs full of water, she got fresh air! All around, above and below her, the cataract splashed and thundered. By a miracle, the bubbles and spray provided enough air to let her breathe. Dorothy thought, *Somebody will find me before it is too late.* She tried to get into a more comfortable position and relaxed.

Meantime her friends, thinking that if she had gone over the falls, perhaps her head had struck a rock and she was lying stunned at the bottom of the pool, broke branches off the trees and probed with them. But they could not reach bottom.

Edmund Pennybacker, a husky lad from White Plains, New York, dived repeatedly into both pools, then said, "Say, she might be right under the falls. You guys hold me and I'll have a look." But before he could submerge in the fast water, he was swept from their grasp, and disappeared. Now two of them were gone.

A moment later, young Pennybacker showed up in the lower pool, rubbing his bruised shin and blubbering, "Holy mackerel! There's a funnel down there, and I was sucked clear through it. But I didn't find Dottie. She must be under the upper falls."

And she was, with the blood running to her brain and her body getting numb from the cold. Slowly the roar of the falls became fainter, the queer yellow light above her face turned black and Dottie, for the time being, passed out.

It seemed to her terror-stricken friends as if help would never come. Ade Nitschelm had sent two men to notify the forest rangers, fire department and state police. They found that the White Mountain forest fire crew had been called to fight a woods fire in Maine. And the Conway fire department was battling a $50,000 blaze that was sweeping the Lucey farm.

State Trooper Kenneth Hayward was speeding to the Lucey farm fire when he heard over his car radio about the accident at Swift River. He turned and raced to Rocky Gorge.

By six o'clock, all kinds of help had arrived: the emergency crew from the Public Service Company, the forest rangers, and the rescue squad of the Conway fire department with ladders, ropes, and grappling irons. As more than an hour had gone by, it was assumed that Dorothy Sparks must be dead. They decided to divert the course of the stream to lessen the amount of water going over the falls, and to drag there.

A truck was sent to get potato sacks and shovels, and a crew was set to work cutting brush and rolling rocks into the stream. By the time the truck had returned, and the sacks had been filled with sand and placed in the river, twilight enveloped Rocky Gorge.

Men worked feverishly with picks and crowbars to dig a new ditch to divert the water to one side. Ever so slowly, the twelve-foot waterfall diminished, and the foamy white water at the foot of the falls became clear.

Other men moved quietly, lowering and lifting their poles through the water. They lashed two poles together to make one long one, and fastened a blunt iron hook at the end. They had wanted to use the new, sharp grappling irons, but Trooper Hayward persuaded them not to, saying, "What's the sense of mangling her? Think of her folks."

Once, Merton Yeaton thought he had hit something but the iron came away clear. And in her watery prison, Dorothy Sparks came to when the grapple scraped across her knee. She tried to grab the iron, but could not reach it. Terrified, she thought, *What if they don't come back!*

Then the grappling iron caught again, and when Yeaton pulled it up, a small piece of pink cloth clung to the hook. Passed from hand to hand, it was identified as part of Dorothy's bathing suit, and news that her body had been located under the falls spread rapidly through the crowd.

Now the question arose: would they attempt to get the body out that night or wait until morning when they could see better? They decided they might as well finish the job.

Firemen came running with ladders. Ade Nitschelm brought his beach wagon close, to carry Dorothy's corpse to the morgue. Dr. Charles E. Smith, deputy medical referee, who would have to sign the death certificate, watched from the bridge. Portable floodlights were assembled and hand-held flashlights winked through the darkness.

Some time after eight o'clock, more than three hours after Dorothy Sparks had disappeared, Chick Whitcomb saw a hand moving back and forth under the surface. He called for a stick with a noose, and managed to loop the line over the lifeless wrist. It tugged and held, and drawing the rope taut, he handed the pole to a fireman, saying excitedly, "Hang on to it! If we lose her now, she'll be gone for good!"

Trooper Hayward grabbed Whitcomb by his belt, others held his heels, as he plunged his arm into the icy water to grasp a small, stiff hand. The fingers closed around his!

"I've hauled many a drowned person out of the water," he said later, when I interviewed him, "but that was the first time a corpse ever shook my hand!"

Whitcomb held on to the girl's hand and kept pulling. Yeaton and others reached in, and slowly Dorothy was eased to the surface. In the eerie shadows of Rocky Gorge, the slim, nude figure looked like a marble statue as it was raised to the top of the ledge.

Then Dorothy Sparks opened her eyes, her lips parted in a little smile, and she flung both arms around the state trooper's neck!

She was carried to the beach wagon and taken to the North Conway Memorial Hospital. Her bruised knee and ankle were bandaged, and she was given some orange juice and a light sedative. Snuggled down in her warm bed, she slept soundly.

After a version of this story appeared in *The Reader's Digest* (Drama in Real Life, March 1949), it seemed as though everyone wanted to know how badly Dorothy Sparks had been injured.

Well, I saw her card at the hospital, which read:

> Dorothy Sparks, Media, Pa.
> Admitted July 20, 1942 9:15 P.M.
> Discharged July 25, 1942 (five days later)

[244]

Dr. Charles E. Smith of Conway, who attended her, told me, "She had a lame foot . . . and the muscles of one ankle were weakened. There was an abrasion on the knee cap. She shouted until she lost her voice, so her throat was a little sore. That's all."

I met Dorothy herself in the North Station, Boston. I had already visited Rocky Gorge, measured the falls and talked to a dozen or so persons who had helped in her rescue; I wanted to hear her side of the story.

After we had talked for two hours, I asked if she had any bad effects at all. "Oh, no," she said. "I have been a lieutenant in the WACS since then, and more active than I ever was."

She was returning to her home in Media, Pennsylvania, after a vacation in the White Mountains. So I said, doubtfully, "I don't suppose you went swimming in the Swift River?"

"Oh, but I did, several times." And then she added, "But when I crossed Rocky Gorge, I used the foot bridge!"